100
Reasons
To *KEEP* Him
100
Reasons To
DUMP Him

Sharon Naylor

Gramercy Books
New York

This 2000 edition is published by Gramercy Books™, an imprint of
Random House Value Publishing, Inc., 280 Park Avenue, New York, NY
10017, by arrangement with Three Rivers Press, a division of the Crown
Publishing Group, a member of Random House, Inc.

Gramercy Books™ and design are trademarks of Random House Value
Publishing, Inc.

Printed in the United States of America

Text design by Mercedes Everett
Cover design by Studio Graphix, Inc.

Random House
New York • Toronto • London • Sydney • Auckland
http://www.randomhouse.com/

Library of Congress Cataloging-in-Publication Data

Naylor, Sharon.
    100 reasons to keep him, 100 reasons to dump him / Sharon Naylor.
        p. cm.
    Originally published: New York : Three River Press, 1997.
    ISBN 0-517-20965-9
Man-woman relationships—Miscellanea. 2. Men—Psychology—
Miscellanea. I. Title:
    One hundred reasons to keep him, one hundred reasons to dump him.
II. Title.

    HQ801 .N39 2000
    306.7—dc21

                                                              00-061745

                      8 7 6 5 4 3 2

To Sarah, Katie, and Madison

Acknowledgments

Many thanks to my editor, Shaye Areheart, and her capable staff, as well as my agent, Elizabeth Frost Knappman.

Special thanks go out to Karen Beyke and Joanne Blahitka for sharing their best Keep Him/Dump Him stories and advice.

Author's Note

The suggestions in this book are purely for enter-
tainment value. By no means should you dump
your current boyfriend or divorce your husband
just because he never brings you breakfast in bed.
And you shouldn't keep a lying, cheating felon
just because he does.

Nobody's perfect. But you can hope for the best.

100 Reasons to Keep Him

He gives hugs out of nowhere.

You're doing the dishes, just minding your own business, and you're embraced from behind. When he walks into the room, one of the first things he does is put his arms around you and pull you near to him. He just *loves* being in contact with you.

Some men *accept* hugs, and some give them when the occasion calls for it. They seem neither happy nor comfortable with the obligatory squeeze. You've had hugs from this type of man before. You're at full embrace, and he only has his arms stiffly around the *perimeter* of you. Like he's hugging an atom bomb. He pulls away, and he looks like an unhappy schoolboy.

A real man, one that gives true meaning to the phrase "one to hold on to," is not only comfortable hugging you, he also likes to do so as often as possible. Or, at the very least, he initiates as many hugs as you do.

He just can't keep away from you.

$\mathcal{H}$e loves his mother and his sisters.

You can always tell a good man by the way he treats his mother and sisters. If he adores them, then he adores women. He's been raised to respect women, to value their work, to treat them right. He's been raised with a consciousness of the female mind, perhaps raised not to be afraid to show his own feminine side. These, by far, are the conditions that create the best of men.

If he's patient when he's on the phone with his mother, keep him. He has a good heart.

If he says "I love you" to his sisters once in a while, keep him.

If he does favors for them, like picking up show tickets or watching the kids as a last-minute replacement sitter without a grumble or tirade, keep him.

If he speaks kindly of these important women in his life, if he remembers their birthdays, then he is a man who has the capacity to love you with all his heart too.

Keep him. He's a good man.

He takes care of you when you're sick.

The goodness of your man's heart comes out when you need some tender, loving care. And there's no greater time for that than when you're sick.

When you're ill, he orders you to bed. For rest, not sex.

He's a walking encyclopedia of home remedies and doctors' orders. He makes you a big pot of chicken soup—he gets the same credit whether he makes it from scratch or just opens the can—and he warms up your tea every ten minutes.

He goes out to get you every magazine you requested, even if he has to run all over town to find last month's issues. He goes back out five minutes later to get you more cough drops or tissues.

He takes your temperature and makes sure your environment is warm and cozy. He keeps track of your medications and calls the pharmacist to ask about drug interactions and side effects. He calls your mom for you and asks her about your symptoms.

One of the real tests: He doesn't mind if you get sick on or in front of him. Now that takes a large degree of dedication and a good heart.

He cares for nothing more than how you're feeling, how he can make you comfortable, how he can make the pain go away. He fields your phone calls, keeps annoyances at bay, and snuggles up to you in bed as you sneeze and wheeze your way through the night.

You feel better just having him near you.

$\mathcal{H}$e writes great letters.

Communication is the key to any successful relationship, so it's a very good sign if your man does not resist expressing himself in more than one medium. Any man who puts pen to paper to express his true feelings is willing to share himself with you, to allow his innermost thoughts to flow out and reveal themselves to you. And even if all he writes about is how great you looked this morning, it's still reason to rank him right up there with the great minds of civilization.

A man who writes great letters can make the heart swoon, misspelled words and all.

So what makes a great love letter? He could be the author of an epic account of his love for you, or he could just scribble a quick "I Love You" on a napkin. It doesn't matter. If it makes your heart beat just a little bit faster, makes you sigh, or sends you to Cloud 9 for the day, it's a work of art. And so is he.

Your grandmother would have loved him.

Grandmothers can be pretty selective when it comes to your significant others, but if you're sure your grandmother would have loved him, then he's a catch.

If you're lucky enough to have a grandmother in your life, see what she thinks of him. No one wants more for your happiness than she does, and if she approves, you have yet another seal of approval. A grandmother's love is never blind.

A good rule of thumb: If she cooks for him, invites him to dinner, or asks you about him a few days after they meet, he's passed the grandma test.

If, like me, you feel she's smiling down on you from heaven, keep him.

$\mathcal{Y}$our dad likes him.

An even tougher sell than Grandma, Dad's out to protect his little girl. So if Dad's pleased with the initial handshake, the looks of him, his job, and all the other prerequisites, chances are he's either a really good actor or a really good catch.

Do yourself a favor and *don't* coach your guy before the big meeting with Dad. Don't tell him to call your dad "sir." Don't tip him off as to your dad's favorite teams and players for guy-type small talk. Just throw him in there and see if he floats on his own.

How will you know if your dad likes him? He'll offer him a beer before he goes and gets one for himself. He asks his opinion and advice on everything, from stocks to sports. He'll put his hand out first to shake when your guy is leaving. He trusts him enough not to quiz him endlessly on the evening's plans or ask the last time he got his car tuned up. Because if Dad senses that your guy is a keeper, then Dad also senses trouble. He could lose his little girl.

He gets just a little bit jealous of your guy friends.

You've known your guy friends forever. They could be your old high school buddies, the guys from your dorm, friends from work, or your childhood buddies from the neighborhood. You've never dated any of them, no matter how gorgeous they are, and you love them like you love your best girlfriends. Your guy, though, has to figure out how to deal with it when he comes over at midnight and your guy friend is there, munching on a pizza with you. He has to gauge his reaction when your guy friends hug and kiss you good-bye.

If your guy gets "that face," that accusatory I-know-you-two-did-it face, then his green eyes are likely to be a problem. But a guy worth keeping will believe you the first time. He'll *like* your guy friends because they're important to *you,* and he wouldn't dream of giving you the old them-or-me ultimatum.

If he gets just a little bit antsy at some of those guys' visits, late-night calls, even what he suspects are longing looks and flirtatious contacts, it's just because he knows *you* are the catch and that any guy in his right mind would want you. A little male insecurity is a good thing at times; smothering jealousy is not.

$\mathcal{H}$e stays awake to cuddle.

Keep him, keep him, keep him, if he's a cuddler. Think about it. Do you really want a man whose idea of physical intimacy is a few minutes of performance and a solid eight hours of sleep in the same bed?

A man worth keeping is one who holds you when you want to be held, one who believes that being physically close is every bit as good as being close in your hearts and minds, one who caresses your back without being asked to.

He'll stay awake after sex, perhaps getting playful, tickling you, laughing with you. Maybe he'll even initiate another round, or at least be *conscious* when you do. That's physical intimacy.

If the nicest feeling in the world is snuggling together, all enveloped by his arms and his body, keep him. If you roll over for Round Two and he's not in REM sleep, keep him.

He doesn't change the subject when you talk about kids.

Some guys run screaming from the room when any sentence contains the words *kids, someday,* and *Wouldn't you like to have?* (Some run screaming when those singsongy kids shows are on television, but that's understandable—evaluate the situation closely.)

A priceless guy loves kids and would love to have a set of his own someday. He loves his nieces and nephews and your friends' kids. He doesn't roll his eyes and slink away when your pregnant friends come over and start talking about the joys of motherhood.

He tells you that you'll be a wonderful mother. Maybe in the same breath, he confides that he knows he'll be a wonderful father. He can't wait to teach his kids to play soccer. He wants his kids to have it all, great schooling, a great house in a great neighborhood, great toys he can enjoy too, a puppy, a Range Rover for family vacations.

He'll go with you into the baby section to pick out baby gifts for upcoming showers and kiddie birthdays, and he'll stay in there without looking sheepish and uncomfortable. He'll go to couples' baby showers with you, good-naturedly taking part in those silly shower games.

The idea of procreating doesn't scare him, and the idea of procreating with you doesn't scare him off.

If you can see him handing out cigars with little pink ribbons on them, or even if he just smiles and looks with interest when you show him those cigars in the catalog, keep him.

He tells you that you look great with no makeup on . . .

. . . and he means it.

He'll look at you when you're starting to apply your face, and he'll say with complete honesty, "You know, you don't need any of that stuff. You're beautiful without it." If he thinks you're a natural beauty, then he's naturally a great find. He loves you for who you are underneath the things you put on to decorate yourself.

Pity the poor woman who has never let her husband see her without makeup on in thirty years. Pity the woman whose man goes on a talk show to complain that she never wears makeup for him anymore. These are people whose relationships are just that . . . topical.

Your guy, in thinking that your skin is even more lovely without layers of concealer, foundation, powder, blush, pencil lines, and shades of plum raisin is interested in you. He loves you with your face paint and without it.

With him, you don't have to be a work of art or a constructed fantasy woman. You can just be you, and if you don't have time to curl your lashes and apply two coats of mascara in the morning, you don't have to hide from him. And you'll spend far less on cosmetics in thirty years than that woman on the talk show.

He reads the articles and books you save for him.

A friend once bought a best-selling author's relationship book and gave it to her guy when their relationship started to hit a downward spiral. She asked him to read the book so they could work out their problems. When after a month he hadn't read any of it, she went through and folded corners on the pages she really wanted him to read. Again, after some time, he hadn't picked up the book. She went through and this time highlighted specific lines of advice from the book, so that it would only take her guy about half an hour to get the messages he needed to work with her on the relationship. Again, *nada*. Before she resorted to writing the lessons out on his toilet paper, or dropping quotes at the dinner table, or playing subliminal tapes in his car, she dumped him and was glad for it.

A keeper will take interest in what you have to show him. He'll pick up the book and check it out; or, if he truly doesn't have time, he'll commit to a time frame, such as "Next weekend, I'll be able to start going through this." He'll recognize it as important, and value the fact that *you* would like him to take a look.

A guy worth having is one who will agree to work on the relationship even when he personally sees no problems with it. You don't need an expert to tell you that.

*H*e drives slower when you ask him to.

If he's got a lead foot or a secret dream to drive in Indy, chances are you've white-knuckled your way through what was supposed to be a relaxing Sunday drive. But what separates the Dream Man from the Speed Racers is his ability to take his foot off the gas when you make a simple request to slow it down.

He doesn't take it as an attack on his masculinity.

He doesn't call you a big chicken.

He doesn't go off on a tirade against women drivers.

He just slows down. Because he knows it makes you more comfortable.

Now that's a guy worth keeping.

He'll cry with you at sad movies.

I personally would worry about a man who doesn't cry when Old Yeller or Bambi's mom are killed.

A man who cries at sad or touching movies has sensitivity and compassion. He feels things and isn't afraid to share those feelings with you. He isn't afraid to let you see him be human.

He's your Partner in Sniffles at the movie theater, handing you the clean popcorn napkin so you can dry your eyes.

He won't hide his red, puffy eyes from you or anyone else as you walk back out through the lobby when the picture is done.

He'll hold you while the *Beaches* tape rewinds as you wail about the funeral scene.

He'll tear up at the same scene of a movie you've watched together over and over. It just gets to him, and he doesn't mind if you know it. Be glad you have a man who knows how to express actual feelings. Be glad he's comfortable enough with you to let himself cry.

Be glad he'll watch those kinds of movies with you, and he doesn't require any explosions, martial arts, or chain saws in the only films he'll sit through.

If you can watch anything with him, keep him. If you hear him sniffling on the other end of the couch, hold his hand and keep him.

He describes you to his friends as talented, intelligent, and classy before he gets to sexy, hot, and has great legs.

If he goes around telling everyone about your best qualities, the first ones on his list are probably the first ones in his own lineup of priorities. Of course, any man lucky enough to have you is going to brag about everything from your brains to your bottom, but where he *starts* says a whole lot about him.

So what's first on his top ten list about you? If character traits outnumber body parts, keep him.

$\mathcal{H}$e creates inside jokes with you.

Having your own little language, your own little cues and jokes, is something that's yours alone. It says you're so happy together that you can create your own form of communication, complete with lots of laughs and maybe a blush or two.

Of course, you risk being the annoying couple with the secret giggles, the baby talk, and the personalized songs you've rewritten to suit the two of you. So what? Let the other people raise their eyebrows. They only wish they could be so cute and so together.

Acting goofy is just a revisit to the exciting times of young love, and it makes being in a relationship *fun*. So if he can laugh and play the wink game at parties, if he's not afraid to sing your version of childhood songs in front of your friends, and if you're always smiling, keep him.

$\mathcal{H}$e knows all of your favorite things.

He knows what kind of yogurt you like, and which kinds make you sick.

He knows your favorite bands, your favorite color, your favorite suit.

If he's asked by a relative what you want for your birthday, he's able to do more than shrug and mumble, "I dunno. Ask her."

When he's out at the store, he'll pick up your favorite candy bar and a two-liter bottle of your favorite soda. And he gets points not only for doing something sweet for you but also for having the presence of mind to know what you like. It means he's been paying attention, and that your preferences matter to him. He's noticed. He pays attention because he wants to give you what you want.

So the next time he doesn't have to ask, tell him how much you love it that he already knows. And tell him you'll keep him.

He always makes up with you on the same day.

Among the many snippets of advice we get from relationship experts and moms and dads who've been married for forty years: Never go to bed angry. Never let that little fight—no matter how minor—sit inside you and come to a slow boil as you lie awake at night with as much space between you as possible.

The guy worth keeping is going to want to resolve the fight quickly, to talk it out, resolve, and then say I'm sorry. He's not going to be the type to stomp around the house, slamming doors, and giving you the silent treatment for the weekend. The guy worth keeping is not that much of a baby. He cares enough about you to get rid of whatever's bad between you and get back to being close and happy. So he'll do whatever it takes to get there, even if it means sitting up for hours and going over the issue until you're both happy.

He's genuinely unhappy when all is not well. Fixing it is a priority.

So if your guy doesn't let the fight escalate, and you're always at least civil by the end of the night, then be grateful you have a guy who knows how to say, "I'm Sorry."

$\mathcal{H}$e shows you the funniest comics while he's reading them.

If he interrupts *his own* reading to show you the funniest comic strips in the Sunday paper, he wants you to smile. He wants to share that little burst of happiness that just made him laugh.

Those interruptions could be annoying as you're trying to find your mutual fund listings in the financial pages, but try to see it for what it is . . . your guy is sharing the little joys in his life with you. That's a big payoff.

He gets points also for clipping out his favorite comics and either sending them to you or hanging them up on the refrigerator. Cuteness factor: writing your names in the dialogue bubbles to personalize the messages. Say it with me . . . *awwwww*.

Women say the most attractive thing about a man is his sense of humor, and if he's willing to share his with you, or at the very least his appreciation of humor, then he's a keeper.

$\mathcal{H}$e shows off in front of you.

Could he be any cuter than when he flexes for you in his underwear? Is he the most wonderful man alive when he sings to you?

He preens, he struts around, he acts like the male primate he is, all in a mode of courtship you might hear discussed on the Discovery Channel. If you analyzed him for being this adorable, the anthropologist in you would call it a mating dance. But when he comes out of the kitchen, proudly displaying his chocolate soufflé, it's just too fabulous for words.

What's better than a man who shows off for you? He's the guy on the dance floor who—if he had his pick of anywhere in the world to be, it wouldn't be there—is dancing his way through the macarena. He's the guy who plays a little too eagerly in the company softball game and then is sore for days afterward, but, hey, he caught that would-abeenahomer shot just at the fence. He's the guy who's trying to show off at tennis and tells you he's just got to warm up before he can *really* start playing.

It doesn't matter if he's Andre Agassi on the court or John Travolta on the dance floor. His showing off for you doesn't have to mean he's great and perfect at everything. He just wants you to think he's great, and if he's willing to flex in his underwear for you and, for heaven's sake, do the macarena at your cousin's wedding, then he is.

He gets into all the television shows you like . . .

. . . and he doesn't fake it. Countless guys attempt to get high marks with their girlfriends by sitting with them through an episode of *Melrose Place,* spouting off little catchphrases they read in a men's magazine under "What to Say to Get Her to Sleep with You." You can tell if a guy doesn't *really* watch *Melrose*.

Your wonderful guy *will* get into the shows you love, just as he'll encourage you to get into his favorite programs. He'll start to get to know the characters' names, and he'll even get a high five for correctly remembering a character's former husband and last season's sweeps-period storyline. "Hey, didn't she try to kill him last month?" will get a man a serious boost in his own ratings, especially if that didn't appear in any television listing or article recently.

The closest of couples can make viewing a favorite show a part of their weekly ritual. Let the critics say what they will about couch potato lifestyles. A good must-see show gives you something to talk about, even something to learn from. When your favorite characters have relationship troubles, you can see a part of your own relationship in there. If he says, "She was wrong to kiss that other guy," then you know where he stands. You know he'd never do that to you.

If you can share a good cop drama together, or a Discovery Channel marathon, plan to spend many television seasons with him.

$\mathcal{H}$e knows which towel is yours . . .

. . . and he keeps his hands off it. He knows how you like him to hang up his towel when he's done (that is, just hang it up *somewhere*; don't leave it on the ground), and he respects your wishes about the cap on the shampoo, the hair clippings in the sink, the toilet seat in the down position.

If you can share a bathroom with him, you're miles ahead of most other couples.

He doesn't say, "That's women's work."

He doesn't expect you to cook every meal.

He doesn't leave the laundry and the ironing to you every time.

He knows how to run a vacuum and does so often.

He can get a stain out just as well as you can.

Everything formerly known as "women's work" is just work to him. He's an equal-opportunity Dustbuster.

He knows you were not put on this Earth to clean up after him, and he'd laugh just as incredulously as you if someone were to say that a woman's place is in the home/kitchen/barefoot, etc. He doesn't want a maid, and he doesn't want his mommy. He's a can-do guy, and no realm of the house is off-limits to either of you.

So if he does his own hemming and gets the rust stains off the bathtub, keep him.

He has a job . . .

. . . or at least serious prospects of getting one soon.

A big part of his entire identity is going to be what he does for a living, like it or not. And even though this economy isn't kind to many people, sending many out of work and keeping many others from getting the jobs they desire, it's still a good indication of his worthiness if he at least has short-term and long-term goals and is actually doing something about them. They may be realistic and attainable, sure, but they also may be way out there. As long as he has some kind of picture drawn for himself. As long as you've seen him circling classified ads and actually trying, not just lounging on the couch spending your paycheck on pizzas and pay-TV.

If he's got a great job and he's good at it, people respect him, and he's a straight-up employee, then he's the shiny penny in the job pool. Dive in and grab him up.

Your job is every bit as important as his.

He doesn't get that look of only-borderline interest when you talk about your day.

He's interested in your projects, often asking you how it's going with the new account, the new boss, the new client.

Your office party is just as important as his, and if the two fall on the same night, you go to both.

He talks about your job with as much pride as he talks about his own. He's really impressed with your work and with the path you're cutting for yourself in the office. And when you're mad about some workplace injustice, he's on your side.

He's your job cheerleader, telling you that you can do it, encouraging you to give it your all, and understanding when your job gets in the way of his plans.

He helps you with your research, reads over your notes, helps you plan the big meeting.

And if your work is at home, whether in a home office or staying home taking good care of the family, he's every bit as proud and supportive as if you had to go out there wearing $30 pantyhose and $300 suits every day.

If he supports you in your life's work, then keep him forever.

$\mathcal{H}$e looks adorable when he's sleeping.

He looks so peaceful, so angelic while he's sleeping there. You look at him in the moonlight, and he's just so beautiful. Sure, his mouth may be open and he may be making those nose-whistling sounds, drooling on the pillow, and carrying on a conversation in his sleep (which you instigate by asking questions that he answers in his sleep, so you can kid him about it in the morning). Who hasn't admired their guy in such a state?

If you look at your guy and his expression is one of utter peace and contentment, you know that you are part of the reason he sleeps so soundly. Not because you're *boring* to him, but because he hasn't a care in the world. Your life is great, and as you watch him sleep, you know that wonderful dreams are floating through his head.

So if your guy looks like a vision of serenity as he's lying there in the bed, cherish the look of him. If he's just lying there snoring and making those nose-whistles, stick your fingers up his nose. That ought to stop it.

He's so cute when he's sick.

He's just so pathetic, lying there in bed moaning about his flu symptoms.

The patient in him brings out the little boy, so gentle and appreciative of any comfort you might bring him. He does as he's told, drinking his tea and eating his chicken soup, staying in bed and promising to get a flu shot. He sleeps a lot, which means you get to peek in and check on him, and all your sympathy makes him that much more precious to you.

You get to help him, to return the favor when he took care of you during your last bout with the flu, and you're there to welcome him back to normalcy when he's feeling better. It's a cycle of ups and downs, some of that in-sickness-and-in-health that brings people closer. It helps to be close to someone when they get sick in front of you.

If you find yourself not minding that much, and if helping him get better is important to you, then keep him. Keep him at arm's length so you don't catch what he has, but keep him anyway.

*H*e dislikes the people who are mean to you.

He's never met her, but he hates your Aunt Zelda. She's always mean to you at family parties, after all, playing up her own kids' accomplishments and insulting you for yours (i.e., "Doesn't using all that paper in your architecture office *kill* all the trees in the world?"), forgetting birthdays and anniversaries and harassing you for forgetting hers, just generally being an evil woman.

Your guy has had the great luck never to run into old Zelda, but he hates her *for you*. He agrees with you when you rant about how she yelled at you for offering her a chocolate because you're trying to kill her with the sugar. He tells you not to invite her to Thanksgiving dinner. Basically, he helps you dislike her.

So what if you're supposed to love all people, forgive and forget. Aunt Zelda is mean, plain and simple. And your guy makes you feel better about not having to keep kissing her butt your whole life.

He also hates the high school chums who tortured you, the guy who stood you up in college, your old prom date, the intern who got you in hot water at work. He's on your side, always, and he lets you get it all out.

Of course, when he meets Aunt Zelda, he's going to be sweet as pie. He's not a Neanderthal, you know.

He lets you have the biggest slice of pizza.

Pizza is a defining topic in most relationships. If he's the right man for you, he'll do the following:

He'll ask you what toppings *you* want on it.

If he likes hot, hot, hot peppers on his pie, he'll order them on the side so none get on your slices.

He lets you have the pieces with the air bubble.

He'll make sure you get as many pieces you want *before* he polishes off the pie.

He'll let you have the last piece.

Or at least, he'll cut it in half so you can share.

If he's got good pizza etiquette skills, then you're all set. Keep him.

He'll tell you when there's stuff in your teeth.

You're both so natural together that it's not an embarrassment. That's why happy couples can tell each other when they have stuff in their noses, bad breath, eyeliner smudges, and all those other unpleasantries. A guy worth having will not let you go off from lunch and back to the office with spinach in your teeth. He's not going to let you go through your day looking like a raccoon when your makeup smears, and he's not going to avoid the awkwardness of telling you that you need a breath mint.

He'd rather do it than have you embarrassed and humiliated later.

If this guy cares about you enough to hand you a Certs with an understanding smile, then keep him. You'll return the favor someday.

He admires you from across the room.

Even in a room filled with beautiful people, sparkling crystal, and priceless art, you're still the most interesting focal point for him. From across the crowded room, he catches your eye, sending you a smile, a wink, or a nod.

He makes you feel wonderful, and you know he'd rather be talking to you than with anyone there, even the blonde in the red dress.

Longtime couples have crowded-room signals, like a tug on the ear for "I love you," a switch of the glass to the other hand for "Save me from talking to this creep," a slow bite of a canapé for "Let's go home and make it a private party." He's sending you an even bigger message by admiring you from across the room: He loves you and wants to be with you. Quick, grab that canapé.

He takes magazine quizzes with you, without arguing.

"What's Your Sexual Signature Style?" "How Does He Rate in Bed?" "Is He the One?" "Is He Cheat-Proof?" The quizzes in the magazines are laughable to most people but can be a lot of fun, though some guys hightail it out of there whenever any mention of quizzing and grading their performance and personality comes up. Your perfect guy, though, laughs right along with you while you're circling your As, Bs, Cs, and Ds. He may even go get the pencil.

He probably knows how to give the "correct" answer, according to what the magazine editors would say rates the highest. And he can always laugh off the results.

Any guy who's willing to sit down and subject himself to the questions in "Does He Know What He's Doing in Bed?" just because you like taking the quizzes, loves you far more than you know. Keep this guy.

Your pets love him.

If Fluffy warms to him instantly, then you know he's either a good catch or he's had salmon for dinner.

Pets have a sense about people. They seem to know when someone is a good soul, a gentle and caring person. That's the person they let rub their bellies and cut their toenails. They'll jump up and sit with him on the couch instead of their favorite place: in your lap. In minutes, they'll have him wrapped around their little paw and cooing at how adorable they are.

If your guy wasn't so great, you'd have a dog that barks at him, a cat that hisses and hides under the couch when he's around, goldfish that float belly-up at the top of the tank (okay, that *may* be from something in the water or the fact that you left the tank unplugged for a few days). Your pet loves you and wants you to know if this guy checks out in the world of animal instinct.

So when your dog nuzzles up to your guy's leg, it's either a sign of approval or . . . something else.

He stays with you even after your
most embarrassing moments.

You got drunk at the office party, jumped up on the
desk, and sang to the entire company. He stayed by you.

You went to a smorgasbord, overstuffed yourself, and
had to run to the ladies' room after that one . . . last . . . piece
. . . of . . . German . . . chocolate . . . cake. He stayed by you.

You fell down the stairs at the stadium in front of all his
friends, spilling $30 worth of sodas and hot dogs. He picked
you up, dusted you off, and stayed right there.

Basically, no matter how many times, and how many
ways, you embarrass yourself, he's still right there. A lesser
man would shy away from your limelight, but he's there
right alongside of you, and he assures you that no one will
remember a few years from now. Make that a few decades
from now.

He'll say, "No, you're not fat," as many times as it takes . . .

. . . and may he be richly blessed for it.

Your great guy knows when you really want to hear that your insecurities are unfounded and that you're as beautiful on the outside as you want to be. He knows that your eyes can sometimes be like those warped mirrors at the circus, the ones that make you look short and round.

Best of all, he'll say "No, you're not fat" endless times. Over and over, every time a too-snug shirt makes you feel bulbous, every time a supermodel prances across the television screen and you've got a pint of ice cream in your hands. He'll assure you again and again, never sighing or rolling his eyes, never saying, "Will you stop it already? *You're . . . not . . . fat!*"

By the look in his eyes, by the way he admires you, belly bulge and all, you know he believes it. You're really not fat. That shirt just shrunk and that supermodel never knew the joys of superfudge chunk with white chocolate and raspberry swirls. She also doesn't have a guy as great as yours. Share the ice cream with him, hold him close, and keep him.

*H*e doesn't blame his childhood.

Some guys blame every problem they've ever had on an inattentive father, an emotionally abusive household, social and economic hardships. The list goes on. Then the guys who've *really* had a tough life, complete with death and destruction, go along fine without blaming a soul for how they turned out.

If your guy doesn't point the finger, doesn't tell you his mom ruined his life, and doesn't nod along at talk shows that do the same, he's apt to be a pretty well-adjusted guy. If he's proven that he can take responsibility for the choices he's made, he'll also accept responsibility for the choices he makes regarding you and your relationship.

And, in the near future, he won't be blaming you for everything *you* do to mess up his life.

He gets uncomfortable when another woman flirts with him.

Guys are adorable when they get the kind of attention from another woman that they would have loved to get when they were single. Call it guilt, call it fear. They just look so scared, so afraid that maybe they did something wrong.

He doesn't enjoy flirting with other women. He likes flirting only with you. That's far better than if he were the type of man who thrives on getting those sultry stares from women in bars. Those are the type of men who only know that one way to boost their self-esteem. Your guy doesn't have that problem. *You* boost his self-esteem.

Some guys find it just *icky* when your friend flirts with them. They get all flustered, and you can smile, knowing they can be trusted.

Especially touching is the phone call your guy will give you if he's been out with his buddies and another woman came onto him. He tells you exactly what happened, even if he ran away from her before she could say hello. He's too sweet for human consumption.

If you're the only woman he wants brushing up against him out at a club, then he's a keeper.

He saves your letters.

They don't have to be bound with pretty red ribbon and kept in order in a shoe box under his bed—I'd worry about him if he did that. It's just nice to know that he wanted to keep the letters you sent him. It's nice to know that when he's missing you, he might pull them out and read one or two again to cheer himself up. Romantic guys are like that.

Keep him and his letters, too. Your kids will get a kick out of them someday when they read them without your permission.

He thinks.

A man's mind is his best asset. If your guy is smart, if he has opinions and thoughts on various subjects, and if he impresses you with his knowledge, then he's a man with substance. A man who thinks can be passionate about things. He believes firmly in some causes, and he's able to match wits with you when you're having a real discussion. He doesn't have to be Oxford-educated. The topic of the day could be anything from the state of the defense budget to the new fast-food burger. As long as he believes in something, he's worth having a lifetime of conversation with.

If your guy answers your questions with something more than "I dunno, what do you think?" then he's keepable. If seeing things through his eyes gets you thinking and analyzing, if he can get you to consider a valid point that's the *opposite* of one you've always supported, then he's got a lot upstairs for you to discover. A thinker is a good catch, and there's something sexy about the *intellectual* brand of stimulation.

He has a great voice.

His is the voice you want to hear in your waking moments and deepest dreams.

His whisper is sexy, his first groggy words in the morning are sexy . . . even the way he calls the dog is sexy.

A man with a voice like that can send chills up and down your spine. In a good way.

You love to hear him talk, and he knows it. His "romantic voice" always gets you in the mood; his "innocent" voice always gets him out of trouble.

It's the voice you're most happy to hear on the other end of the phone.

Think . . . is this the voice you want to hear forever? If yes, then keep him.

He actually wants to do a couple costume on Halloween.

That is, he's a good sport. If you have your heart set on going as a pair of dice (as in "Paradise"), he'll go along with it and stand there while you fit him for his big, square cardboard box. If you're more into the sultan-and-the-harem-girl getups, he'll gladly sport the turban and go bare-chested in the brisk October weather. Anything to make you happy.

Your great guy's not going to scoff at your ideas, forcing you to back down on them so you can go as something a little less conspicuous, like baseball players. He's going to wear that costume with a smile, knowing you'll be the cutest, most clever couple there. After all, it's only one night, and it'll make you happy. Just no pictures, please.

*H*e calls you outside to see the rainbow.

If your guy is a sweetie at heart, he's going to think of you whenever he sees your favorite things. And when he takes the dog for a walk and an enormous rainbow appears overhead, he'll cut the walk short and come back to get you because he knows you love them. He gets extra points for making any kind of comment about you being the gold at the end of the rainbow. A bit cheesy, perhaps, but he's got good intentions. *And* he's walking the dog without being asked.

He checks out the house when you hear a noise.

Old-fashioned as it may be, it's still comforting to have him around the house when you hear a noise in the middle of the night. Sure, he may take you with him when he goes room to room, searching for intruders. Sure, you could probably do far more damage to anyone who did break in, but it's nice to know he's willing to take a look. At least you're not alone.

Believe it or not, there are guys out there who would just send you and the cat, and then roll over and go back to sleep.

Your great guy is willing to go downstairs and close the spooky storm door that the wind just blew open. He's willing to fumble around in the dark for a flashlight when the power goes off—hitting his shins on the coffee table as he goes so you don't have to hit yours. He'll go down in the basement at night even when the lightbulb burns out and it's just too scary down there to get the clothes out of the dryer.

What a guy. What a hero.

He kisses it and makes it better.

There's something about a kiss on a sore knee that makes the injury seem to heal much faster. If your guy comes home to find you sidelined by anything from a broken leg to a paper cut, he'll be right there with a kiss and an ice pack.

His presence makes the hurt go away.

He cheers you up and makes you smile, even if he is good-naturedly poking fun at you for *how* you broke your leg or risked all to get that paper cut.

He's not overly sensitive.

A sensitive guy is good to have, but your guy is not sensitive to the extreme. He doesn't take every comment you make as a personal attack. He doesn't think the world is out to get him. He doesn't berate himself, he doesn't dwell or obsess, and he doesn't make you walk on eggshells so as not to offend him.

Instead, he knows how to make lemonade out of lemons, he can bounce back, and he knows that life's not trying to beat him down. And he can take constructive criticism when you offer it.

He wears a decent bathing suit.

None of those thong bathing suits for him. Or the little European briefs. A keepable man knows enough about fashion and public decency to prefer bathing suits that are more of the boxer variety. He knows to let his appearance be assumed, not shrink-wrapped.

Enough said.

He doesn't make you say things twice.

Why is it that the average guy tunes out in the middle of your conversation? Why do you have to repeat everything? And why does he let you finish a story and *then* say, "I'm sorry, I wasn't listening. Could you give me that last part again?" That's the last part all right, buddy.

A guy worth keeping will actually listen. And absorb. And comprehend. And remember. He'll look up from his television show long enough to listen to you say something. He'll be able to recall the conversation you had last week about what to get for his brother's wedding.

A guy worth keeping will make you feel far from ignored.

He shows you nerdy old pictures and videos of himself.

He doesn't mind if you see him during his tight-fitting jeans period. He doesn't mind letting you see him with long hair. He'll laugh along with old family movies of him doing a spastic dance at the family reunion. (That videotape could be worth some money!)

He's not afraid to show you where he's been and how much he's improved since then.

So if he's willing to let you see how he used to look, if he *wants* you to see how he used to look, then you have a man who doesn't want to hide anything from you. What in his life could he want to hide more than his old prom photos? Did they actually make tuxes like that? Did they actually make eyeglass frames that ugly? And who was that girl? Was her dress low-cut enough?

And to show your love for him, your trust in him, and your unwillingness to keep things hidden, feel free to pull out your old junior high school pictures. Show him every bad haircut, every nerdy first-day-of-school outfit, every hammy shot you took. And if the two nerdy kids you were in those pictures would have looked great together, keep him now.

*H*e supports your diet, but he doesn't bug you if you fall off of it.

There's a fine line between being a diet supporter and a great big nag. If your guy knows how to encourage you to keep at your diet and fitness plan, then he's helping you with your goals. He doesn't ask why there are no more sandwich cookies in the cupboard when it's obvious you had a little slipup. He doesn't toss you a big guilt trip for giving into a small fries when you're out to lunch. And he doesn't raise his eyebrow at you over the dinner menu, warning you away from anything that sounds remotely good.

He just cheers you on when you go out for your power walk. He tells you that you look like you lost weight when you did. He brings you a fruit plate when he goes to the kitchen for his own snack. He says "keep up the good work" when you're sweating away on your treadmill. He celebrates your goals with you, and he helps you bounce back from the little pitfalls. His support pushes you through plateaus, and his pride in you is part of your motivation.

And if he's willing to try your exercise tapes with you, just stifle the smile and keep him.

He doesn't compare you to his mother.

It's okay if he says your spaghetti sauce is just as good as his mother's, but it's not okay if you're always getting comments like, "Can't you iron my shirts like my mom did?" "This isn't the way my mom makes barbecued pork sandwiches" and the ever popular "You sound just like my mom."

If your guy can tell the difference between you and his mom, and he likes that there's a difference between you and his mom, then he's normal. If he doesn't dare to hold you up to comparisons or measure you against anyone else, then he appreciates you for who you are, not because you'll fill his previous caretaker's shoes.

Keep making the barbecued pork sandwiches your own way, and hold on to him.

He reads.

You have to love a guy who reads. Whether it's a good mystery novel, a magazine, even the Sunday paper. A guy who wants to expand his mind is not going to turn into a lump who's fed his information by the television. A guy who reads is less likely to be one of those zombies who tunes you out when the flickering light of TV mesmerizes him. A guy who reads is likely to be as smart as you are, as willing to discuss things as you are, and he can read the things-to-do notes and shopping lists you give him before he goes out.

He tells you his dreams.

Think about it. A guy who tells you exactly what he dreamed last night is actually opening up the door and letting you into his subconscious mind. From what he tells you, he knows you can tell exactly what he's thinking. He has nothing to hide. He's not worried about you knowing his secrets.

If he tells you he dreams of *you,* then keep him. Whether you believe him or not. He still gets points for being sweet enough to say that.

He doesn't mind if you haven't shaved your legs.

So what if you give him a little stubble burn under the covers? A guy worth keeping is not going to demand that you be primed and perfected every minute of the day. He's not going to shrink away from you, demanding that you go do something about those legs or he's just not going to touch you.

A guy worth keeping is going to love you on stubble days and all.

You get hugs and kisses every day.

If your guy comes up and plants one on you out of nowhere, he's a sweetheart.

If he rarely leaves the house without kissing you good-bye, or if the first thing he does when he comes home is kiss you hello, keep him, keep him, keep him. He just *loves* to kiss you. He doesn't shrink away from kisses, he doesn't give you that "why are you kissing me?" look, and he doesn't have any problems with kissing you in front of other people. His passion for you overrides all things.

Now that's a guy worth keeping.

$\mathcal{H}$e's good in an emergency.

Again, he's a hero type. But this time, he's the guy who has the quick reaction time, who will dive into the pool fully clothed to save the drowning child. He's the guy who jumps up to give the Heimlich maneuver when everyone else is stunned, just watching.

He's the guy who runs the show when the ambulance needs to be called and keeps everyone else calm while he starts the CPR. He's got a cool head in an emergency, and he knows just what to do.

When someone else has an emergency, he's right there with the offer to drive out and pick them up. He'll take a neighbor's child to the doctor. He'll pick up a relative from the airport, even though he planned to watch the big game.

In an emergency at work, he's the guy they call. He can fix the problem without spinning out of control. He's the go-to guy.

And in your own emergencies, he's the one you want right there to help make it all better.

He remembers birthdays, anniversaries, and special days.

A guy who remembers your birthday all on his own, without your having to remind him or write it on his calendar, is a guy worth keeping. He also remembers your anniversaries—even of the first time you saw each other/met/kissed/ate Chinese food, etc.—and loves to celebrate them with you.

A guy this great may even come out with "Do you know what today is?" and you may not even know. As long as it's not his ex's birthday, he's a dream.

Do you know how many women would *love* to have a man who consistently remembers special days, who is prepared ahead of time, even? Do you know how lucky you are? Don't take this presence of mind on his part for granted. Wish him a happy anniversary, and hold on to him.

He has female friends.

You know from your own male friends that they're the greatest guys in the world, and you hang out with them for that very reason. So if your guy is the kind of guy in whom women trust and confide, then he's a winner. He knows how to treat women. He has many of them as his equals in his life.

Of course, they all may be secretly lusting after him, but tough. He's yours.

He'll stay up if you can't sleep.

A guy who sacrifices part of his own eight hours of sleep just because you can't drift off is a keeper. He'll turn on the light and talk to you. Maybe he'll suggest some warm milk or a snack, even bringing them to you in bed.

He's not going to tell you to go out and watch TV and quit keeping him up. He's not going to whine and moan that he's going to be so tired tomorrow. He's not going to sigh dramatically and tell you what you shouldn't have had for dinner. He's just going to sit up and stay with you until you get tired. You could use a little quiet time together anyway, he reasons. And if he suggests you spend the time talking about your relationship, your future—as long as it's good news—keep him!

*H*e can handle talk of female medical issues.

He's not traumatized when you tell him your annual pelvic exam went well today. He can listen to news reports about mammograms and menopause. Even those yeast infection commercials don't throw him.

It's your body and your health, and he just wants to know that everything's fine with you.

A guy worth keeping sees you as a person, not just a bunch of body parts, some with weird stigmas attached.

Hey, if he can get through those yeast infection commercials without cracking an embarrassed smile, chances are good he can handle a conversation about ovulation.

$\mathcal{H}$e thinks deadbeat dads are the lowest form of life.

Does it make him mad when the news reports another case of fathers not paying child support? Does he think that's just incredibly low and irresponsible of any man to refuse to support his own children? Grab him right now and kiss him for having such a good heart.

The same goes for anyone who cheats on a partner. Does he think they deserve everything they get when they're caught? Is he glad when *television* characters get busted for committing adultery? This just tells you how he feels about the subject. He values loyalty. If cheating makes him this sick, then you can pretty much bet that he's not going to do it to you.

Keep him.

He loves to watch you get dressed.

Watching you move is his favorite thing. He loves to admire you as you slip on your little black dress and carefully apply your makeup.

Men are fascinated by this little ritual of ours. (Maybe that's why so many try it themselves!) Face it, we do have more fun getting ready for an evening out, and your guy loves to watch you prepping and primping. He loves to watch your slow transformation from beautiful to drop-dead gorgeous, and he knows that he'll be peeling you out of that dress later that night.

So if he's sitting back on the bed with a little pleased smile on as he watches you zip up your dress, give him a little wink in the mirror. He's just enjoying how beautiful you look. Let him know he doesn't have to say it. You already know.

Then it's your turn to watch him dress. Enjoy it. You'll be peeling him out of that suit later anyway.

He gives you more than one drawer at his place.

If he's not stingy about giving you some space, then he's welcoming you into all of his. A great guy will give you your pick of the drawers, a full half of the closet, prime space in the medicine cabinet. He'll let you stock your goodies in the fridge, and he makes room for your makeup next to the sink. Since he really wants you there to share his life, he's willing to share his square footage.

And if he gives you the best toothbrush holder slot, he's a keeper.

He knows which songs remind you of other people.

Your guy knows to turn the channel whenever a particular song comes on.

It's not as if your guy is afraid you might still carry a torch for any of your exes. He just knows what associations those songs bring to you, and he'd rather not send your mind off into the past. He wants you right there in the present with him, so that you can make history with your own songs now.

He just knows that if he comes into the kitchen humming a song, it had better be the one that makes you think of *him* naked.

Just the fact that he considers your feelings is a big plus for him. Dedicate a song on the radio to him, and have the deejay say you'll keep him forever.

He doesn't laugh at your beauty regimen.

As much as guys love it when we outline our lips and line our eyes, there's usually a reason we use the hot wax and the upper lip bleach behind closed doors. Some guys just don't get it. But not your guy. If he comes home and your face is covered with three different kinds of creams, he doesn't roll on the floor laughing hysterically, making any jokes about creatures from lagoons. He just kisses you on a noncreamed spot, asks how your day was, and tells you that you don't really need all that because you're beautiful the way you are.

He may even get a rise out of watching you hot wax your legs. So let him watch. As long as he doesn't laugh. Not only does he love you, he appreciates your tolerance of pain.

If he's worth waxing, tweezing, and bleaching yourself for, you already know he's worth it. So keep him.

$\mathcal{H}$e doesn't give you "that look" when you spend too much money.

Whether it's his money or yours, some guys raise their eyebrows at you and try to make you feel guilty for buying that sweater on sale. Money is a loaded issue, one that most people fight over all the time.

But if your guy isn't the type to control you, if he doesn't expect you to ask permission to use the plastic, then you're in the clear.

You know your guy is the greatest if he can rationally discuss money with you but isn't afraid of a little discretionary spending. He likes to be impulsive, and he lets you be impulsive with him.

Sure budgeting and keeping a level head about the finances is very important to your lives, but he knows it's just fun to come home with a new toy every once in a while. Maybe more than a few toys once in a while. Maybe half the makeup counter at Estée Lauder. But who's keeping track? There's still enough to make the bills and the savings, so live a little, you say. And he does.

If the two of you can balance the financial planners with the social directors in you, then you both have the right person.

Keep each other.

He's so cute when he's trying to find the right tie.

Isn't he adorable when he's trying to put together the right outfit?

Does he have to worry not only about what matches but also about the right colors and fabric for the season? No, honey, you can't wear your gray wool suit to the outdoor wedding this weekend. Sigh . . .

Of course, he may have a better fashion sense than you do, but it's still fun to watch him take out all of his ties and hold them up to himself in the mirror. It's still fun to watch him squint at his reflection, trying to figure out if that's navy or black.

And it's so adorable when he just can't find the right outfit and he comes to you for help. The striped tie or the solid? You look great in both of them, sweetheart. But go solid.

Watching men dress and greeting them when they come out of the room all spiffy and smelling so strongly of their freshly applied cologne is so unbelievably enjoyable, it's a wonder you ever get out at all.

If he cleans up real nice, keep him.

*H*e actually uses the gifts you get him.

All of the shirts, the classical music tapes, even the gag gift boxer shorts with the little pineapples on them—he uses them all because they came from you. You could get him the goofiest birthday present and it will never end up in the bottom of the closet, unseen until garage sale time.

Even if he doesn't see the beauty in the item at first, like that painting you got him for the hallway, he'll display it anyway. Because it came from you.

Which means now you actually have to wear that blue sweater he got you last Christmas.

He can live if he misses a game.

He wouldn't miss your family party because the game is on. (He knows he can try to sneak in one of those minitelevisions so he can watch under the table with the rest of the guys).

He doesn't get mad because you made unmovable plans on Sunday, when you know Sunday is game day. And he doesn't expect you to leave him alone all through baseball season, which never seems to end.

He can live if you're both late getting home and the game's already started, or if the cable goes out and he's going to miss the whole thing. He doesn't storm out the door and drive across town to the sports bar to watch it there.

If he gets to see the game, great. If he doesn't, it's not the end of the world. He can catch the reruns on the news later. Or you can tape it and watch it together later.

There's nothing wrong with him if he's a sports fan. But he should know enough to put the game in the right slot on his priorities list once in a while.

His touch sends shock waves through you.

He could just be putting his hand on the small of your back while he reaches around behind you for something in the kitchen drawer. But just his touch sends electricity through you. You remember how exciting it was the first time he held your hand or touched your face. And you still feel that now.

If just a second of physical contact with him is enough to make your heart rate rise, he's a keeper.

You find yourself smiling whenever you think of him.

You're driving to work, thinking of the great card he gave you last week, and you find yourself smiling.

You could be flipping through a catalog, surfing the Internet, waiting on hold with the insurance company—if thoughts of him enter your mind, a wide smile grows across your face, and you just can't keep it back. He just does that to you.

You could be way past the point of teenage infatuation, you could be together for years, you could even be so used to each other by now that everything's routine. If it still makes you smile when you think of him, keep him.

He's got a clean record.

If he's wanted in seven states, maybe you shouldn't keep him. Maybe you should turn him in.

But if he's an upstanding sort of guy, a model citizen with a clean slate, then he's all yours.

Public Enemy Number One may not always be there for you when you need him. But your Good Guy always will. Keep him.

You would have dumped him in high school for being too nice.

It's a law of nature. The nice guy finishes last. And in high school, all the girls would practically knock the nice guy over to get to his friend, the dumb jock or the big jerk.

It's only after graduation, maybe at the five-year reunion, that we see the nice guy is the one we should have been after. He may not have had the chiseled jaw and the great hair, but he was always nice and funny. The teachers loved him, and he went places in life. He became the kind of guy every woman dreams of once she gets past her Dangerous Guy Period in her twenties. He's the guy you want to keep, the guy you're sorry you ever passed up now that you know better.

So if you wouldn't have looked twice at him while you were at your peak immaturity, if you would have been shocked and disappointed when *he* was the one who called to ask you to the prom, if you ever told him then that you liked him, *but* . . . back then, he was the nice guy you always wanted for yourself. You're all grown up now, so you know enough to keep him.

$\mathcal{H}$e's a man of the 1990s, not the 1950s.

He doesn't expect you to bring his food to him.

He doesn't leave his plates on the table for you to clean up.

He doesn't say he's the boss of the household.

He doesn't expect to rule the household, reigning over all decisions.

He doesn't expect you to ask his permission for you to do as you please.

He doesn't yearn for the old days when men were the boss and women stayed home.

Instead, he's a man of the present who believes you're his equal in all ways, and that the people from the television shows during the 1950s and 1960s were frightening.

He's a one-woman man.

You're his one and only. You've never been so sure of anything in your life.

If he's staying true to his promises to be faithful to you, then he's a man worth keeping. His honesty and loyalty are some of his best traits, and what could be better?

He loves you, so he's not even looking around. Keep this man.

He says "I don't deserve you," but he does.

There's nothing like a little humility to endear him to you further.

When he looks into your eyes and says those words, you get to kiss him and convince him that yes, he does deserve you. And you deserve him.

A man who says he doesn't deserve you is also saying that you're so fantastic he can't believe he actually has you. You could eat that up with a spoon, couldn't you?

Let him be a little in awe of you now and then, but always bring him close and tell him you love him. He deserves that as well.

He calls when he says he will.

And he shows up when he says he will, too.

He's worth keeping when he delivers on his promises, even little ones like I'll call you tonight.

He would never dream of leaving you waiting by the phone, possibly worrying about him, and he would never, never stand you up. You don't have to deliver the speech about him lying in a ditch somewhere, bleeding to death. He wouldn't put you through that.

He doesn't have to be punctual, to the second. Just as long as he comes through.

If you can count on him, keep that reliable guy.

He never cancels.

He's far from the type of guy who would cancel plans with you if something better came along.

If he did have to give you a rain check for dinner, it's for a good reason. His grandmother is in town and he's taking her to lunch. That's a good reason. His cat is having kittens and he wants to be there to give her water with an eyedropper. Another good reason.

His buddies are having a keg party? Not a good reason. Your guy wouldn't dream of it.

A guy worth holding on to keeps his word. He goes along with plans even if he doesn't really want to because he knows you've done the same for him.

He keeps the plans he's made with you because he *likes* doing things with you. Being with you is fun. Nothing better could come along.

Think back on your history. Has he always canceled out for a good reason? Give him credit and keep him.

$\mathscr{H}$e respects you.

He treats you with respect when he listens to what you have to say. He considers how things will affect you. He thinks about what's important to you.

He honors your decisions, and he listens to your side, even if he doesn't agree.

He'll work on the problem, even if he doesn't think there is one.

He respects you as his equal in all areas.

He would never call you names, never raise a hand to you, never do anything that would earn him a spot on a talk show as "A Dog."

If he treats you as you wish to be treated, keep him.

$\mathcal{H}$e says, "I love you," every day.

It's the last thing he says before he leaves the house. He doesn't hang up the phone unless you've both said it before "good-bye." He just says it out of nowhere, for no reason. And he means it.

He doesn't have to *say* it to say it, either. He could say it without words by a simple caress or embrace, a meeting glance, a smile, or picking up a pint of frozen yogurt just because he thought you'd like it.

He loves you.

Keep him.

He calls you his best friend, too.

Your guy is a keeper if he's also your friend. More so if he thinks of you as his friend, too. You're truly close if your relationship brings you to a point where you *like* each other while you're loving each other. There is a difference.

If you're as close to him as you are to any of your best friends, if you have just as much fun and just as much genuine fondness for him, keep him. If he feels the same way about you, and tells you so, give your friend a hug and keep him.

Every time is like the first time.

If he can make you feel *that* good without the benefit of First Time Fever or the lure of the forbidden, even after all this time, don't even question it. Just keep him.

Unless your first time was really, really bad, or you got arrested or something. If every time is like that, then it's time to see a therapist.

He doesn't call to check up on you after girls' night out.

You've known guys like this before. If they don't *show up* during girls' night out—either you see him hiding across the bar watching you or he feigns his innocence: "What are *you* doing here?"—your phone is ringing when your key is in the door. You get the third degree and then you have to feel guilty for having a great time without him.

Your guy would never do that. He trusts you. You can go out with your friends, and he doesn't have to interrogate you when you get back. He knows you have a life outside of his, and he lets you have it.

Your great, keepable guy is content with asking you, "Did you have fun?" He doesn't have to put you under a bright spotlight, pressing you for exactly what you mean by that. He's sure enough of himself and he's sure enough of you to be glad you had fun.

And if he does show up at the same club, by true coincidence, send over a drink and flirt with him mercilessly. Why should your friends have all the fun?

He's everything you've ever dreamed of . . .

. . . and more.

If you looked back in your diary, way back in the fifth grade, you just wanted a guy who was going to be nice to you, who wasn't going to pull on your braids, who was going to laugh at all your jokes, and be so handsome he could be on the cover of *Tiger Beat*.

In your high school diary, you lamented that there are no nice guys left on earth. You just wanted someone who was smart and funny and cared about things and would never lie to you or dump you for someone with a bigger chest.

In college, you wanted someone who wasn't going to stand you up, who was intelligent and compassionate and kind to all people. You wanted an accomplished man who respected you and believed in your work and identity.

In your most pleasant dreams, you see the perfect guy. And it's your guy. He's everything you ever wanted, and many more things you never even knew you wanted.

He may be a little too old for *Tiger Beat* (On second thought, if Luke Perry could be on there just a few years ago while in his thirties, why not?), but he's your Dream Guy. And you don't even have to enter a sweepstakes to talk to him on the phone.

He's the best thing that's ever happened to you.

Relationship-wise.

He's the greatest guy you've ever known, the most romantic, the sweetest and most gentle.

He makes all the other guys you've ever dated look like sawdust in comparison.

Your friends wish they could find a guy as great as yours.

Your parents consider him part of the family.

He's just . . . the greatest. If you can't find another word for it very easily, just let a contented sigh do the talking for you.

*H*e's the first thing you want to see in the morning . . .

. . . and the last thing you want to see at night.

You want his eyes to be smiling at you when you wake up, and you want his voice to be the last you hear before you slip off to Dreamland.

You just want to look across and see his head on that pillow. (Provided the rest of his body is attached. This isn't *The Godfather,* after all.)

Waking up to him means you're bound to have a good day, and ending your day with him next to you means it was perfect.

You can tell him anything.

No subject is taboo with him. You can talk about his family, his childhood, his old girlfriend. You can talk about religion and child rearing and the state of our country.

You can tell him all the secrets of your past and trust that he'll keep them.

You can tell him about a family secret, and trust he'll keep that, too.

You can tell him about your darkest days, and he'll still love you for getting through them.

You can tell him what you wouldn't dare tell your parents, your sister, or your closest friends.

Anything. He'll keep his word. He'll keep your confidences.

If he's a man you can talk to, keep him.

He makes you feel alive again.

You didn't think you could ever feel so wonderful. Maybe you had love once, lost it, and thought your chances were over. Now you have him, and you feel like your life is magical.

He's brought back the little bits of excitement that fill a functional day with sparks and electricity.

He reminds you that you are a vibrant person, and he makes you feel young.

You have an energy you didn't have when it was just you, your other single friends, the couch, and the television.

You feel like you're taking in twice as much air when you breathe.

Colors are brighter, the birds sing louder—your life has been digitally remastered for greater viewing pleasure.

He reminds you of your own potential, which was inside you all along. It's a gift he helps you find for yourself. Keep him.

He doesn't mind if you're not in the mood.

Sex is something you're supposed to share, not supply for him.

If he's fine with waiting until tomorrow, then he's someone who knows what making love is all about.

Your great guy isn't one of those boys who gets mad and tells you that you'll feel better afterward—like being with him is now a painkiller. Your guy doesn't say, "Okay, we'll just kiss then," and slowly start to continue, hoping you'll change your mind once your hormones kick in.

He just takes no for an answer, like all good men do.

$\mathcal{H}$e gives to others.

Charity, to him, is not just a big tax write-off. He's glad to drop some money in the bucket. He loves fund-raisers and walkathons, and he'll call in his pledge to the telethon.

His old clothes go to the shelter. He volunteers his time where he's needed.

He expresses interest in building houses for the homeless, working for others, helping where he can.

He's the first guy to lend out his car when his brother needs it, and he'll help his friends move into their new house.

He'll work a double shift or overtime to cover for someone with a personal problem.

He's a giving guy. The type of guy everybody counts on and calls on because they know he'll be there. That could be a pain when you can't make plans because he's committed for the month, but you know to appreciate that quality in him. It's what makes him so great.

*H*e can laugh at himself.

And he reminds you not to take life so seriously. He's not the type to brood for weeks over some bad turn of events. He doesn't agonize over the play he didn't make during the game or the boss's criticism of his last project.

He can laugh at himself when he knows he messed up. He can laugh at himself when he has an embarrassing moment. He can laugh at himself when he knows he's being cranky.

And he can get you to laugh at yourself and lighten up.

He's not a ball of tension. He knows that laughter makes your steps through life a lot easier, and he helps you along your journey.

He'll drive for hours to see you.

He gets the same credit if he just drives across town in the rain. If he wants to be with you so badly that he'll make the trip even when it's not so fun, then keep him.

If your guy would drive for miles—he may not *have* to, but he would—if he would brave the harshest weather and take public transportation to get to you, then he's a guy worth holding on to. (You may have to ask him to pick you up someday when you're stranded out of town, so this is a plus.)

He doesn't mind getting older.

As long as he gets to do it with you.

No middle-age crisis for him. He's happy with you and the comfortable lifestyle you have. He doesn't need the eighteen-year-old and the sports car. Well, maybe the sports car, but that would only be to take you out in style.

The specter of being thirty, forty, fifty, sixty . . . doesn't scare him. He knows that when he starts to fall apart, you'll be right there falling apart with him.

He doesn't worry about the phone bill, as long as he gets to talk to you.

To him, it's worth every penny just to hear your voice. He doesn't rush you off the phone or limit you to discount hours. He doesn't set an egg timer by the phone.

A guy who *wants* to talk is every woman's dream. He's communicating, sharing his thoughts, laughing with you, and listening to you. Can you really put a price on that?

Just make sure there are no 900 numbers on the bill, and you're all set.

His gifts have more meaning than price.

He's not the kind of guy who thinks more is better, pricewise. He doesn't believe he could show you how much he loves you by maxing out his credit card for you.

He says much more by writing you a poem, framing a picture he took of you, saving a bottle of sand from your vacation and later making you a little "beach" during the depths of winter because you said you can't wait for the summer.

A little plastic ring from a box of candy is just as touching as the real thing. The music mixes he made for you are straight from his heart.

He could spoil you with priceless trinkets and expensive dinners out, but he knows a meaningful gift has no price tag. And it's the one you really wanted anyway.

He brings you breakfast in bed.

The toast is done just the way you like it, the eggs aren't runny, he used the heart-shaped waffle iron, and there's a flower on the tray.

It may not happen on any day but your birthday, but he thought enough to want to pamper you. He wanted to do something special to make your day, to start your celebration off with a little romance.

Is he the greatest, or what? Sigh.

He lets you have the aisle seat.

He knows where you're most comfortable, and he wants you to have that.

He'll switch seats with you when a big-haired lady sits in front of you at the theater or when the brat behind you is kicking your seat.

He'll take the cramped backseat in your friend's convertible if you have to be in the front because of your tendency to get carsick. He'll let you stretch out during long flights while he's stuck in the middle seat next to the big guy with the newspaper.

He's proof that chivalry isn't dead yet.

Keep him.

$\mathcal{H}$e supports your decisions . . .

. . . without thinking, "How does this affect me?"

If your big promotion means moving to another city, he's not going to give you the guilt trip about the distance that will be between you. All he cares about is your vice presidency. You'll make the distance thing work.

When you have big decisions to make, he's there to support you, not to affect them. He knows they're just that—*your* decisions. And he respects that.

Who he is inside matters more than what he is on the outside.

He has a good soul. He's a decent person. He's fundamentally good.

And that matters so much more than whether or not he has a chiseled jaw, his own law practice, and a Jaguar.

It's his spirit that makes him worth holding on to.

It just feels right.

You have no nagging doubts, no uncomfortable moments when you wonder whether or not you're doing the right thing.

Your gut instinct says that you're in the right place with the right person.

All you feel is comfort, joy, and happiness.

He makes you believe in True Love.

He's proof that True Love does exist for those lucky enough to find it.

You believe that he may have been sent to you through some form of divine intervention, as if you were somehow deserving of this kind of happiness.

True Love found you when he walked in the door. It guided you together and pushed all the right buttons so that you stuck together and formed something meaningful.

Your friends and family hold you up as the perfect couple. If it could work for you, maybe it could work for them. You give others hope that your brand of togetherness is possible, so it's still possible for them.

All the things said in love songs are true of you and him together.

Just listen to the song "True Love" someday. That's why you should keep him.

He's "The One."

Everyone has someone out there who's meant just for them.

Their soul mate.

He's yours.

You are meant to be.

Keep him always.

100 Reasons

to Dump Him

He calls you "The Ball and Chain" or "The Little Woman."

Not only is he unoriginal, he's just not funny.

If this is the way he refers to you when talking to his friends, he's asking people to *feel sorry for him* for having you in his life. Doesn't sound like Prince Charming to me.

If the guy doesn't have a more endearing name for you, tell him to take his poor-me routine on the road.

Your mom hates him.

You'll know if your mom doesn't like your guy. She'll roll her eyes a lot, raise the eyebrow, start mentioning how much she liked that nice boy who took you to the prom. If she *really* hates him, she'll have a special nickname just for him—some variation of Sludgebucket, That Loser You're Always Hanging Around With, and He'd Better Not Be the Father of My Grandchildren.

Mom's dislike for the guy you should dump goes way beyond her usual distrust for any man who takes you away for the weekend. She has utter contempt for this guy, no matter how sweet she is to his face.

She doesn't tell you to invite him to family parties, and when you ask if he can come, she sighs and gives you her patented "Oh, all right, if he must."

Like it or not, Mom was always right about the guys you fell in love with and cried over for days. That's what moms are for.

If she won't hug him good-bye, dump him.

Your pets hate him.

If cute, fuzzy, little Scruffy turns into a snarling she-wolf whenever he comes around, face it. The dog *knows* he's no good for you. If Sheba hides under the bed and won't come out until he's gone, she'd rather hang out with the dust bunnies than the likes of him. Then she'll give *you* attitude all night, saying how disappointed she is in you that you just don't *see*.

Animals have a sixth sense about these things. They warm to gentle souls like yourself, and they just hate people who rub them the wrong way, so to speak.

You know your pets. You can tell when they're happy or unhappy. If they just hate the sight of your guy, dump him. And don't go making excuses, saying that pets are just naturally jealous of anyone who comes between them and their owners. Face it. The dog's a good judge of character. The cat knows about guys. And they both want you to be happy.

He reminds you of your ex.

Maybe they look alike. Maybe they wear the same kinds of clothes, have the same color hair, talk with a southern accent. Maybe they both cheated on you for six months before you found out.

If your guy has a lot in common with the guy you had to get away from, then add up two and two. There's a *reason* you got away from the first loser, so don't feel you're okay by replacing him with a slightly less warped model.

If you find yourself getting mad at the same things with your guy that you did with your ex, having the same fights, giving the same advice, begging for attention and feeling lousy all over again, this guy has too much in common with your previous mistake.

Think back to how you ditched your ex and crown this guy with the same title the same way.

Dump him.

He is your ex.

So it's the second, third, fourth time around, is it? You're just rerunning the entire relationship from good to bad to ugly with the same guy. Get off the Tilt-A-Whirl and try a new ride. Stop going in circles.

Getting back with your ex may work if you've managed to fix the problems and work through your issues. But if it's the same old him and the same old you, move on to the next attraction.

He's sexist.

Does he think dumb blonde jokes are the funniest thing since ... Anita Hill jokes? Please. You're smarter than this.

Any guy who likes to poke fun at women or demean them in any way is a big creep. He's the kind of guy they create in movies so they can kill him off and make all the women in the audience cheer and pay another $7.50 to watch again with a different set of girlfriends next week.

A guy who thinks it's funny to make fun of women isn't all of a sudden going to treat you with equality and respect. A man who thinks women belong not in executive positions but at home giving him children is not going to support and celebrate your promotion. Especially if you outrank him now.

If you're embarrassed to bring him out with your girl-friends because you always have to apologize for him later, just dump the ape and find someone from *this* decade to hang out with.

He's racist.

A man with mean comments is a man with a mean heart. Get rid of him and make your world a better place.

He changes the subject whenever you start talking about marriage.

Or any other kind of commitment, like just seeing each other exclusively, cutting down his number of other lovers to "a handful," what have you. . . .

If you've been with this guy awhile and he's *still* afraid to up your relationship level a notch, then have a talk with him. You might just need to work out some issues, maybe communicate until he decides to overcome his fear of growing up and getting serious. But if he's not even going to consider it—he wants to play a while longer—then change the locks.

You'll know you're headed this way when you bring up the issue of marriage, say, at a friend's wedding or while watching a great romantic movie, and he keeps bringing up the Chicago Bulls. "No," you might answer. "A *great marriage* does not mean Jordan and Shaq on the same team." You try to drag him back to the subject, but he's outta there. Bringing up marriage is like bringing up a worst nightmare to him.

Well, end the nightmare. Let him sleep soundly . . . alone.

He changes the subject whenever you talk about having kids.

He's not a big fan of kids? Fine. He'd rather die than change a diaper? Fine.

But if he leaves the room whenever you start talking about how you want to have kids someday—even if you start musing about how beautiful your kids will be someday—you might want to think twice about creating something with half of his genes.

Sure he may not be ready to think about having kids. Many people aren't. But if he can't even face the subject, if he shrinks away from it like a close-up look at eye surgery, and if he can't even indulge you your daydreams, this is a guy who probably doesn't think he should be allowed to procreate either.

When you ask him if you look fat, he laughs and says, "Yes, you do!"

Any guy who doesn't know that the correct answer to this questions is either "No" or "You're beautiful just the way you are" is not worth keeping.

Sure, he may be honest. You may look fat that day, but if he doesn't know you're asking him so that *he'll say no and reassure you,* then you're going to have a hard time getting him to comfort you in life.

Keep a guy who'll love you, extra weight and all. Dump the guy who tells you to hurry over to Weight Watchers as soon as possible.

He tells you to dress sexier.

Warning bells should go off in your mind when he sidles up to you and says, "How come you don't wear those short miniskirts anymore, hon?" If he starts inquiring about your low-cut blouses, your skin-tight jeans, or your microminis, he's either collecting for Goodwill, getting together a wardrobe for *himself,* or asking you to be his own personal playmate of the month.

It's fine to strap on the bustier once in a while, and the miniskirt may be fine for a night on the town. But if he wants you in come-and-get-me clothes twenty-four hours a day, then he's not interested in you. He's interested in your wardrobe.

If he grouses about your leggings and T-shirts, if your birthday gifts *always* come in plain brown-wrapped bags, tell him to take a hike. If he loved you, he'd love you in old sweats just as much.

Your job is just a hobby to him.

Does he call it "Your Little Job?" Does he raise an eyebrow when you talk about your work? Does he think that even though you work an eight-hour day, too, you're *still* able to come home and put in another eight hours running the household and family? "After all," he reasons, "you don't have a real job like me."

Amazingly, there are guys who make *less* than their partners, are in far less prestigious positions, and haven't had a promotion in years who *still* carry around this Neanderthal notion that a man's job is more important than a woman's. If your guy hasn't evolved, show him a glass ceiling of his own. Dump him. Make that . . . downsize him.

He forgets birthdays and anniversaries every time.

It's just not possible for him to remember two dates out of the year.

If your guy doesn't find your birthday or anniversary important enough to write down somewhere, then send him on his way.

The worst offender is the guy you have to *remind,* like you're begging him to remember to get you a card (and then you have to pretend he really means it), and he *still* forgets. This guy's brain is too filled with pointless information, like his old fraternity handshake or the girls from *Baywatch*. There's no room in there for your special days. Save his remaining brain cells the strain. Cancel all future anniversaries and spend your birthday with someone who cares. Not him.

He gives you no advance notice for dates.

He just shows up and expects you to drop everything to go out with him. It doesn't even occur to him that you might have other plans, or that you'd appreciate a little notice. If *he's* available for a good time, well then you must be, too. This is a guy who doesn't see beyond his own world.

Spontaneity on occasion is fine. Surprising you with a special dinner out is fine. But if he's never made plans with you, never given you something to write down on your calendar, then you're a spur-of-the-moment kind of fixture for him.

Tell him you'd like to be asked out on a date once in a while. If he looks at you blankly while he tries to process this information, and then starts laughing and punches you in the shoulder as he says, "Yeah, right. Good one," he probably thinks Wine and Dine is some rest stop on the interstate.

Dump Mr. Goodtimes so you can have something to look forward to.

He's critical.

He cuts down your appearance.

He cuts down your friends.

He cuts down your family.

He cuts down your home.

He cuts down your performance.

He cuts down your personality, your intelligence, your talents.

Please. You have old aunts and bitchy co-workers who can do that for you. Dump him.

He calls to check up on you after girls' night out.

"Where did you go? Who were you with? Did you meet anyone? Who did you talk to? Did you dance with anyone? You didn't go home with anyone, did you? What did you drink? How much did you drink? Where did you go next? Who drove? Did you have fun? More fun than you have out with me?"

Whew! What a pain in the butt.

If he's going to give you the third degree every time you go out with your friends, then he *knows* you're likely to have a good time without him. He just wants to ruin it now so you *forget* how much better off you are without him.

Dump him.

He shows up during girls' night out.

He doesn't trust you out alone with your girlfriends, so he's watching you from across the room. He's sneaking around in the shadows trying to see who you're talking to, who's buying you a drink, how close you're dancing to that other guy.

You don't need the constant surveillance.

And if he *just happens* to show up at the same club, that's fine once or twice. But six weekends out of seven? What a coincidence. The guy's following you. Give him the slip.

He doesn't listen.

His eyes glaze over when you put together more than two sentences at a time. You're two-thirds of the way through your story, and he turns to you and says, "Huh?"

His eyes dart all over the room when you're trying to talk with him, and he forgets what you've said the moment you say it.

When you find yourself giving him little tests, like interrupting yourself to ask him "What did I just say?" or inserting strange nonsensical phrases in your story—he didn't even respond to "Hey, your brother is really cute," and he doesn't even have a brother—you're having to *force* him to listen to you. That's some level of communication you've got there.

If even after your requests the guy can't focus on what you say, absorb what you say, or even repeat what you've said just a second ago, then tell him to take his lack of attention elsewhere. Dump him.

At least if you're alone, no one will be ignoring you.

He says, "We've already discussed this."

But not in a good way. He says it with a roll of his eyes, a slump in his shoulders, maybe a good old-fashioned foot stamp or two. It's the grown-up male equivalent of "But Mo-om!"

A guy worth dumping thinks that the problem is fixed if he yesses you to death while you have a discussion *at* him, and he never has to hear of it again, even if it still bothers you. He hasn't read the passage in the self-help books or even watched the infomercial that says women like to discuss things over and over again until they're resolved. The dump-worthy guy doesn't consider your problem a real problem unless it's his problem, too.

Dump him.

No problem.

He brings up your past.

Not in a romantic way. Not like "Remember when you won that award?" or "Remember when we first met?"

No, he brings up your past not as a party game but as a weapon.

It'll usually start with, "Yeah, well at least I didn't . . ."

Anyone who can hurt you with your own mistakes and worst memories is a guy who's extra dumpable. He latched onto your sore points and knows they're his best way to control you. He makes you sorry you ever confided in him.

If he's going to keep doing this, bring up a bit of his own past. Say, "Hey, remember the last time someone called you a pig and dumped you on your butt and threw you out of the house and told you never to come back? Well, déjà vu. Welcome back to your past."

And welcome to the future.

He talks about his ex.

If you have to hear about her great job at the UN or their trip to Tahoe one more time, you're going to scream. Why does his ex have such a place in your relationship anyway? Why exactly does he tell you all these stories about her?

A couple of tales out of his past are not bad things; he's sharing his life with you. But if you're just being treated to a list of her most endearing qualities while he looks all puppy-eyed and sighs dramatically, send him back to her.

If he's really in love with you, he'd be full of "Isn't she great?" stories starring *you*. He wouldn't need to try to convince you that he's worthy because he was good enough to snag someone as fine as *she* was.

So the next time he starts going on and on about his ex and her family and that weekend in Vermont, just make it the last time you have to hear about any of that.

Make it the last time you have to hear his voice, too.

He calls you his ex's name repeatedly.

Not just once or twice, not a genuine mistake like most of us have made at one time or another. He'll call you her name in the middle of a conversation, then swear you heard him wrong.

He'll *start* to say her name, maybe get out the first syllable before switching to a weird pronunciation of your name.

He'll say her name in his sleep or while the two of you are intimate.

He'll tell you that's the new pet name he has for you.

Hey, if he can't get your name right, and he couldn't even if you were wearing a name tag, then forget about him.

Dump the guy.

He makes your ex look good.

Suddenly, compared to him, your old, lazy, forgetful, boring boyfriend looks like the Catch of the Year. He makes *all* your exes look like princes, and you wonder why you decided to take a step *down* the evolutionary ladder with this one.

If you'd prefer the misery of your last boyfriend over the brand you have with this one, then you're going in the wrong direction. Same if you think of your ex and decide, "You know what? He really wasn't *that* bad."

If you found yourself thinking about *calling* your ex while you're still with this guy, then that's a definite sign.

Anybody who can make your ex look good after all you went through back then is definitely dumpable. Pining for your last broken heart isn't exactly a sign of a healthy relationship now.

Dump him.

It's his way or no way.

He couldn't be more obvious about his need to be in control. To him, if he lets you drive the remote, then he's not the Supreme Being of your Viewing Pleasure.

It's not even an option for both of you to watch *your* shows. You've had to get a second television and go into the other bedroom to catch your own Thursday night lineup.

You have to spend your $7.50 on his kickboxing movies when you'd rather see a romance or a revival.

If your guy is not willing to split the entertainment choices with you fifty-fifty, then he's into his own wants and wishes. You can go on missing your shows, not knowing what anyone's talking about at the watercooler the next day. You can go on squinting at the little crappy television in the other bedroom, trying to figure out what you're watching through the snow and the rolling picture. You can go on saying good-bye at the popcorn counter and going into separate movie theaters.

Or you can dump the guy and not have to apologize for wanting to see the season cliffhanger.

He thinks it's women's work.

He doesn't cook.

He doesn't clean.

He doesn't iron.

He doesn't do dishes.

He doesn't pick up his clothes from the floor.

He doesn't get the newspaper.

He doesn't call to order the pizza or make reservations.

He doesn't get the birthday card for his mother.

He describes anything as "women's work" or "that's your job."

Just because he grew up with a mom who may have vacuumed in a dress and high heels doesn't mean you have to be his personal slave, squeezing yourself into an old outdated model of how a woman is supposed to be. If he thinks certain responsibilities are yours because of your chromosome configuration, then escort him to the door and kick him out.

Dropping the loser is women's work, after all.

His sports come before you.

There's "being a sports fan" and there's "being a sports-obsessed fan." The previous is loyal to his ball club. He'll go to the games. He'll kick back with a cold beverage and really enjoy the matchup. You'll hear him scream "Touchdown!" through the entire house. He may even paint his face the team colors. It's all normal, and you may be just as big a fan as he is.

But when he starts yelling at you because you passed in front of the television and he missed a crucial shot of the quarterback on the phone with the coaching team in the booth, or he couldn't hear the stats on extra points made in the rain during a full moon, think about it.

If he'd rather stay home and watch the game than go to your first big show at a gallery, think twice about it.

If he'd rather go to the second game of the season than take you out for your anniversary, think twice about him.

If Sportschannel comes first, no matter the sport, no matter the season, and if he doesn't respond to you except during commercial breaks, then give yourself a break. Don't be a weekend widow.

If sports aren't something you share, and he's not willing to give you at least equal time, call a time-out and cut him from your lineup. Before you have to put him on injured reserve.

He's not trustworthy.

He blabs about his friends' infidelities to you.

He tells you he was sworn to secrecy, but he'll tell you anyway . . . and you hear him saying the same thing to four other people at the barbecue.

He tells his mother about his sister's sex life, his brother's troubles in law school.

He betrays every confidence placed on him, and you think he's keeping *your* secrets?

There's a little something this guy lacks. Dependability. Perhaps a bit of discretion thrown in there, too.

It's no secret that this guy is worth dumping.

He blames his parents, his childhood, the economy, etc.

Nothing is his fault. Every perceivable imperfection of his is always someone else's fault.

It's not his fault he's overweight. His mom gave him too many candy bars when he was a kid.

It's not his fault he got fired from his job. He was neglected as a child and never learned to be on time and responsible.

It's not his fault he cheated on you. His father was a bad role model when he was a kid.

It's not his fault he maxed out all his credit cards and now has to declare bankruptcy. It's the economy.

Yeah. Right. Sure.

Listen to this guy. He's got an excuse for everything. What was his excuse for not getting you flowers on Valentine's Day? God didn't grow any he could afford?

No excuses. Just dump him.

He's nowhere around during pregnancy scares.

And you think he's going to be around when the test is positive? If the guy can't even go to the pharmacy with you to buy the test, if he's screening his calls when you're one day late, you can pretty much take this as a sign that he's not going to stand by you when he's needed.

Dump him.

He breaks up with you before birthdays, anniversaries, Valentine's Day, Christmas, and other gift-giving holidays . . .

. . . just so he doesn't have to get you a present. Somehow whenever the calendar announces another impending holiday for giving presents, your guy snaps into a cranky mood and he's fighting with you about whatever comes to mind just so you can be too mad at each other to exchange gifts.

I don't think the financial wizards recommend this as a great way to keep your credit card bills down.

If your guy would rather spend your birthday giving you the silent treatment, give yourself the best birthday gift of all. Freedom from him.

He thinks a six-pack is a great gift for you.

Or a ratchet set. Or a big tin of pistachios, his favorite snack.

If your guy consistently gets stuff for you that he loves for himself, and takes for himself, he's not capable of thinking of you.

Of course he may not get you the perfect gift every time. He may forget to give you a gift and *feel awful* about it. Normal guys do that sometimes. But a guy worth dumping is just incapable of asking himself, "What does *she* want?" His mind doesn't expand that far.

To him, the ratchet set is a great gift. He wants one for himself, and hey ... this would just work out great. What good would a bunch of flowers do *him*? They just die anyway, but a ratchet set is forever. Notice that the ratchet set companies haven't adopted it as their big commercial slogan.

If your guy is just beyond being a poor shopper for presents, and he just doesn't care, then dump him.

He never wants to just stay home and be alone with you.

It's not enough for him just to stay home and watch a video or have a nice quiet dinner. He needs outside stimulation, lots of other people, lots of noise, lots of action. All the time. Way past the initial trying-to-impress-you days and into the time when you should be getting cozy and relaxing together.

You've tried to shake off the feeling that he doesn't want to be alone with you, but it won't go away. This guy's idea of a quiet romantic dinner is New Year's Eve at Planet Hollywood.

He can't sit still.

Just talking to you is not enough.

He's not comfortable unless he's in the middle of a large crowd. And if you're there, too . . . okay.

Is this guy afraid of being alone with you? What's the deal?

If he can't stay home, if you two can't just *be together,* then it's clear he's just not getting enough excitement from your life together. If he has to cram it full with parties and dinners and late nights and let's-just-do-*somethings,* then he's not comfortable. And I'm sure you aren't either.

So give him his walking papers.

He'll find something else to do.

He doesn't think.

You've tried not to call him dumb. But he is.

A whole bunch of neurons are just not firing.

Not everyone's a genius. Not everyone's a thinker or the next Great Mind. But he should be able to name more than three states. He should know the name of the president of the United States.

You should be able to use words in the two- to three-syllable range when you're trying to speak with him.

You should be able to communicate with each other at the very least.

If this guy's not on your intellectual wavelength, if he's not on any intellectual wavelength, then just stop calling. He'll probably forget all about you.

He has no opinions.

He doesn't have an opinion about anything.

You're trying to have a discussion about politics, and he shrugs and says, "I don't know."

You're trying to have a discussion about religion, and he shrugs and says, "I don't know."

Music? "I don't know."

Movies? "I don't know."

What would he like to have for dinner? "I don't know."

Unforgivable. Tell him to take his vacant stare and his hollow brain for a long walk. When he asks where, you know the answer.

He's taken over your place.

Suddenly, there are no signs that your place is your own. He's gone from moving some of his stuff in to adding a few decorative touches—to making it look like a *man* lives here—to completely revamping your entire vision.

You just don't feel cozy at home anymore. The few remaining accents that are yours are in imminent danger of being replaced by more of his stuff, until you're afraid he'll completely erase your presence from each room.

Reclaim your space. Dump him.

He pouts.

He sticks out that bottom lip and makes a poor pathetic face until he gets what he wants. It's adorable sometimes. It's all in fun sometimes. The normal guy can use this to make you laugh and lapse into baby talk with him.

But when your guy starts acting like a two-year-old, and those time-outs don't work on him either, it's time to stop responding to "the lip." It may have helped him when he was a child, but he's not a child anymore, exactly.

Dump him.

He's vain.

Forget about what your hair looks like, what does *his* hair look like?

He spends more on personal grooming products than the top six supermodels put together. His cologne collection takes up a whole shelf in the closet. His clothes at retail would take a chunk out of the national debt.

His favorite face to look at is not yours. It's his. He can stare in a mirror for hours. A stray nose hair sends him into a tizzy until he can find his $450 top-of-the-line laser nose hair clippers.

Every woman is looking at him.

Every man wants to be him.

Everybody wants hair as great as his.

Play "You're So Vain" for him and then dump him.

He flirts with other women.

He gets a big rush out of flirting with other women, your friends, your sister, anyone who gives him a passing glance. He may know he's good looking, and he knows that little wink of his *is* very sexy. He does the touch-thing when he's talking to another girl, brushing against her ever so slightly, putting his hand on hers for emphasis. We've all seen the infomercials, the talk show segments, the how-to video.

He loves the attention he gets when he's flirting. And he loves the game of getting another woman interested in him, then dropping her quick because of you when he knows he's won. It's a self-esteem thing with him. Just to see if he's still got it.

So if he feels this good attracting other women, give him the freedom to feel really good all the time.

Then you get to have some fun flirting as well. Just stay away from guys who are "taken."

He compares you with his mother.

Beware the mama's boy! If he's holding you up against the true love of his life, his mother, you're in dangerous waters.

Some normal guys use their moms as references, hoping to see some of the positive traits in their partners that they see in their moms. It's a natural thing. It's a compliment if he tells you that you're the most comforting woman he's ever known besides his mom.

It's not a compliment when he whines, "You're just like my mom."

Spare yourself this argument and the pain of being compared to a middle-aged woman who coddles her son and her poodle and hates your guts. And for heaven's sake, don't try to be like her just to keep him happy.

Dump him. His mama will make it all better.

He thinks "Pudgy" is an endearing nickname for you.

He knows you're not happy about that little spare tire you grew during the winter, and he thinks it's funny to call you Pudgy. Or if you've been thinking of getting a nose job, he calls you The Beak. Isn't he a riot?

It takes a certain kind of guy to pick out his partner's weak spots and use them as a springboard for jokes. A mean guy. A rotten guy.

He might say, "Oh, but I'm only trying to *help* you lose that little spare tire or get your nose straightened. This is my way of *supporting* you."

If this guy can't grow some manners, then dump him. Don't even bother screaming some sort of unflattering nickname out the door after him. You're too mature for that. You can always call him Drool Boy with your friends.

He's a deadbeat dad.

There's nothing funny about a guy who won't support his kids.

Show this guy what real responsibility is. Show him the door.

He brags about his sexual exploits.

The story about the Swedish twins and the hot tub in Aspen may or may not be true. But if your guy has to puff himself up in front of you and everyone else by bragging about his conquests ("Yeah, I bagged her" and other such fineries), imagine how you're going to star in his future tales.

If your own love life is not as exciting as his trips down mammary lane, then dump him. You don't want to be with a guy who's just out to collect good party stories to tell his buddies. You want someone who's going to respect your time together and keep it between you. You want someone who's secure enough in himself that he doesn't need to brag.

Lose him.

You come home and everything's rearranged.

The kitchen cabinets have been completely reorganized (or unorganized). You can't find the juice glasses, and your spice rack is nowhere to be found.

Your guy has rearranged your bedroom drawers so that your underwear is now where your socks were, and your books have been relegated to the garage shelves.

He just wanted to pitch in for spring cleaning? Maybe.

He had to have things *his* way, without a thought that you might *like* your house the way it is? Definitely.

Give him one shot. Tell him you keep the utensils by the stove, not the refrigerator. Ask him to help you restore order. And if he gets edgy, if he gets the shakes until those knives and forks go back to where he had them, do some spring cleaning of your own. Get rid of him.

He doesn't let you see the phone or credit card bills.

Why? Because his girlfriend's phone number is on there? Hotel bills? Charges for flowers that weren't sent to you?

If he's going to hide his finances from you, then there have got to be other things he's hiding from you as well. He's not open and sharing. He's not trusting you with the details of his life. He has secrets, secrets he doesn't want to get busted for, so the bills are for his eyes only.

Some hidden credit card bills are understandable—perhaps your birthday present was charged at Victoria's Secret—but if you're *never* allowed to see the calls he's made, you can do without the secrecy. Dump him.

Your friends roll their eyes when you mention him.

Your friends know what a loser he is, and they hate to hear you talk about him. They've probably been there when he's hurt you. They've listened to you cry over the phone in the middle of the night. They've told you over and over again to dump him.

They know you're smarter than this. You know what they say is true.

Dump him before your friends give up hope for you, and you're left with just him.

Magazine quizzes tell you to dump him fast!

He couldn't possibly have scored any lower on the "Is He the One?" quiz, and he couldn't have scored any higher on the "Is He a Big Jerk?" quiz.

Those magazine quizzes are usually nothing more than just something to do for fun while waiting for your perm to finish at the salon. But sometimes they do point out some universal truths. The general message being to lose the loser and keep the winner.

Take the "Are You Smart in Love?" quiz and dump him.

He has no goals, no job, no ambition.

He just sits on the couch like a slug, or he's Good Time Party Boy with no direction in life other than to Happy Hour.

He's out of work? That's not a crime. Lots of people are today. But if he's *happy* he's out of work so he doesn't have to do anything "not fun," then dump him.

He's probably just sponging off of you.

He's not listening to you when you tell him about a great job interview you could get him.

He's not interested in looking at the classifieds or taking classes while he's got the time.

He's content with his life of leisure.

When you ask him what his goals are, he shrugs.

When you ask him if he's going to think about it, he moves his head so he can watch *The Price Is Right* around you.

A guy who has no direction is a guy who'll take you in that direction with him.

Dump him.

You start wishing he wouldn't stay the night.

"All right, leave already," you're thinking.

You're starting to dread it when he starts yawning and propping up the pillows on what's become his side of the bed. Why can't he just leave?

Not wanting him to stay the night is a sparkling big sign that you don't want to be with him. You don't want something as intimate as spending the night together, sleeping next to each other in peace and silence. That says a lot.

Dump him and get the whole bed, all the sheets and comforters, and the good pillows back to yourself.

He makes plans *for* you, not *with* you.

He accepts the invitation for his buddy's crab feast in both your names. He tells his cousin you'll both be in attendance at her wedding, even when he hasn't checked with you first. He takes over the planning of your social calendar, and you're just supposed to be available when you're summoned.

There's nothing wrong with a guy who likes to plan surprises and big outings where you can both dress up and go dancing. But if your guy is always telling you that you have to be here on this date, here on that date, and no you can't go to your friend's baby shower because he's already committed you for the fishing trip, then it's out of control.

If your guy can't share the date-planning role, and if he's not willing to budge when one of his plans encroaches on your plans, then this is a guy who wants utter control. He wants you to go where he wants, when he wants, and just shut up and be pretty on his arm. Nice.

Dump this guy and open up your entire social calendar.

He's not a man of his word.

You can't count on him.

It can start with something as minor as "Yes, I'll take the dog out after supper," and then it escalates with many repeat performances (or rather nonperformances) until he just doesn't keep any promises at all.

You have to listen to yourself say such things as "But you promised!" and "I'm not going to tell you again!" You're starting to turn into a nag because that's the only way to get things done.

And when he doesn't keep his word, you have to keep it for him. You're fixing the shingles, cutting the dog's hair, picking up the dry cleaning even though you've already been out and it was on his way home from work.

He's forgetful, you say? Write him a list. Give him one of those voice recorder message-taker things so he can hear you giving him his instructions. But if he's not a man of his word, then no amount of coaching is going to do it. He's in his own world and your list of to-dos has no place in it.

The next time he promises to watch his brother's kids, don't bail him out. Dump the kids on him and leave for the day. He'll keep to his word once, so help you.

Then dump him.

He loves the ladies.

He's a cheatin' man? He's not just flirting, he's taking them up on their offers?

Pack him up and ship him out, before you find yourself as a guest on Sally Jessy Raphael.

These days, more than your broken heart is on the line. Cheating could be deadly, and you're smart enough to dump him.

His friends are animals.

He's still hanging out with the buffoons he hung out with in school. They smash beer cans on their heads, belch, and think it's a successful night if they all throw up.

I know you shouldn't expect any man to dump his friends for you, but sometimes you have to draw the line. He crosses it when he turns into another person around his friends. With them, he's loud and obnoxious and crude, making horrible jokes and just being an embarrassment to men who have evolved. You don't even recognize him. He makes fun of you to his friends, and they all call him "whipped" when he sheepishly tries to leave at your request.

You feel like the housemother at a fraternity baby-sitting a bunch of morons. You can feel your own IQ being adversely affected by the company you're keeping. You see his IQ plummet each time his friends are around.

A normal guy will respect your feelings about his friends. At least he won't have them partying at your house all weekend if it's against your wishes. He certainly won't insult you in front of them and he won't pull a personality switcheroo depending on present company. You can forgive a normal guy a few loud friends. A dumpable guy is just more comfortable slopping around with his buddies than standing erect and walking with you.

Dump him.

He threatens to beat up men who talk to you.

He's *that* jealous.

He says he's going to pound any guy who looks at you and he'll kill any guy who touches you. How sweet. You sure can feel secure knowing the Missing Link is in your corner.

A little jealousy is fine in a guy when, after he spots some unsuspecting smooth talker coming on to you, he walks over from the other side of the bar to put his arm around you. Done right, it's kind of flattering. You'd do it yourself if another woman was trying to pick him up at the bar.

A normal guy is no threat. He doesn't rip off his shirt like the Incredible Hulk and smash up the place. If your guy has such green eyes, then get rid of him.

He bugs you about what you're eating.

He knows you're watching your weight, or at least you lamented your thighs last week, so when he sees you open a snack pack of chips with your lunch, he reads you the riot act. "What are you doing? You can't eat those." Either he's Richard Simmons, in which case it's fine, or he's the diet police.

You say he's just helping you, like you asked him to. Fine. But what if you didn't ask him to? And what if he does this when you bite into an *apple* for your afternoon snack? What if he makes piggy sounds while you're diving into the vanilla ice cream? What if he comes in and looks at his watch saying, "You just ate an hour ago!"

There's helping and then there's harping. If he doesn't stop after you ask him nicely, if he seems to be *enjoying* having something else to bug you about, dump him.

He bugs you about what you're wearing.

"Are you going to wear *that*?"

If your guy wants to control even your wardrobe, then this is a guy who sees you as his little puppet. He's pulling your strings.

What you wear is your business, even if you don't have any fashion sense. If you want to dress up, fine. Down? Fine. If you just can't get enough of your tie-dyed stretch pants, fine. You're probably not up for Blackwell's lists either way, so tell him to forget about it. And don't change your style because he says to.

Cut the strings and dump him.

He bugs you about your money.

"You spent one hundred dollars on shoes? What's wrong with you?!"

He sounds like your dad, doesn't he? Aren't you tired of sneaking your shopping bags into the house underneath your coat or breaking the sound barrier trying to get your purchases home before he gets there? Aren't you tired of not being able to wear your new dress because he'd see it? Tired of those guilt trips? Those fights? That look he gives you?

Drop the budget police. Your money is your own. Even if you've splurged beyond belief, it's still not his issue.

Make the next big shopping trip your Freedom Splurge. Right after you dump him.

He embarrasses you in public.

If the strangers on the bus are looking at you like you're crazy to be with him, take the hint.

It may have been endearing at one time that he's so natural, so free, and so unbound by the constraints of human decency and civilized behavior. If so, think about the soundtrack to *Born Free* as you set the animal back out into the wild. His public belching and spitting has got to go. So either he drops the habits you've been complaining about, or it's off into the jungle for him.

His friends come before you.

You have to cancel plans because his friends decided to stay at your place after the game.

He calls to tell you he can't take you out to lunch because he's already at the sports bar with his friends. And you've been waiting an hour for him.

Your crisis can wait; his buddy's bringing over a new girlfriend and everyone wants to check her out.

He keeps you waiting with nothing to do while he chats on the phone with his friends about absolutely nothing.

He acts like a big martyr whenever he does tell them he's going out with you instead. And then he rushes home to meet up with them after your date.

It's nice that he's true to his friends, but if he always sacrifices promises and commitments to you so he can be there for them, then you know the deal. Dump him.

He's banned your guy friends.

He's either forbidden you from hanging out with your guy friends or scared them all away with threats of bodily harm. He's so miserable to your oldest friends that they've lost all hope for you and stopped coming around.

You're not allowed to have guy friends. At the office. At school. In the neighborhood. Nowhere. *He's* the only man in your life.

Stop him before you find him outside in your bushes, watching through the windows.

Reconnect with your best guy friends and remind yourself what a real man is supposed to be.

He blames it on PMS.

Funny how some guys blame everything on that.

They don't get their way? You have PMS.

You're mad that he came home six hours late with no explanation? You have PMS.

A strange woman answered his phone at 3 A.M.? You have PMS.

Yeah. Right. Sure.

Tell him *he* has PMS—Primitive Male Syndrome—and then dump him.

He calls and shows up at all hours . . .

. . . without any consideration to your sleeping patterns or the fact that you have to get up for work at 6 A.M.

He wants to see you, so he figures you should be happy to drag yourself out of bed in the wee hours to let him in and entertain him.

You should be thrilled to death when the phone rings in the middle of the night, which in normal cases would only be a dire emergency, and it's him.

You get the distinct impression he's showing up after his big night out with his friends is done, and now he wants you for a nightcap. Or he didn't get any from the woman he's seeing behind your back, and he's coming over to his sure bet.

Dump him.

You'll sleep better at night.

You always have to be on your best behavior.

You've just never felt completely comfortable, like you could be yourself and it would all still be okay.

You're still measuring your words, worrying if you said something the right way, hoping you hadn't sounded like an idiot just then.

He doesn't give you absolute assurance that you can just relax and not have to "work at it."

It never clicked into feeling right. You've never clicked into feeling accepted for who you are.

That's just a big sign that all is not well. If you can *feel* that it's wrong, then it is.

Save the Miss Manners routine for lunch with the boss or meeting the president. When it comes to a relationship, you shouldn't have to be on your best behavior. Dump him.

Your point of view doesn't matter.

It doesn't matter if you say the sky is blue; he's still going to fight you on it. It's *azure,* he says.

You can have long discussions on your topic of choice, and it's still going to turn out the same way. He's going to take his point of view and make it the only point of view. Yours just doesn't matter.

Aren't you tired of feeling your veins pop out of your neck whenever you speak with him? Aren't you tired of always having to acquiesce to his opinion, just to end the whole debate? Aren't you tired of *him?*

Dump him.

He thinks it's fun to see you mad.

Oh yeah, it's a real laugh riot when you get so steamed at him that you start screaming your head off and wind up in tears. But he seems to get a thrill out of it. He'll tease you mercilessly and actually admit to the people he's humiliating you in front of that "you're so easy to make mad." He's a prince, isn't he?

Who knows what's going on inside his head? Does it make him a powerful guy that he can dig into your weak spots and make you upset? That's what he's trying to do.

Dump him, and find someone else whose idea of great fun is to make you *happy.*

He's a sloppy drunk.

Any kind of alcohol or drug abuse is an irrefutable reason to dump him. Somehow "addict" has never ranked very high on your list of ideal traits in the man of your dreams. But if your guy is just a sloppy drunk on the occasions he drinks, then think about this: Are you enjoying having to clean up after him and apologize to everyone at the party afterward? Do you *dread* this routine every time you go out to a party?

Do you enjoy it when he starts to come down, and he's *mean* all of a sudden?

Do you like watching the transformation in him?

If the man can't control his liquor, and he can't control himself, then it's time to stop playing baby-sitter. Admit it. You can't stop the bed from spinning, and you never will. When he sobers up, dump him.

He thinks birth control is always your responsibility.

He laughs when you bring up the possibility of trying another method, and he looks at you like you're insane when you suggest splitting the cost. Any man who thinks birth control is the woman's responsibility, and any man who refuses to wear a condom and still expects to sleep with you, is someone who shouldn't be allowed to reproduce. Ignorance shouldn't be replicated.

If he's not willing to share the responsibility, stop rewarding him. And dump him.

In this case, holding on to the wrong guy could ruin your life . . . if it doesn't cost you your life.

He has salary envy.

He just can't get over the fact that you're an executive and he's blue-collar. He can't get over the idea that you're making more than he is. He doesn't even want to see your new corner office.

A guy with salary envy is not going to support you as you move up the ladder. He's not going to celebrate promotions. He's not going to give you time to work on a new project uninterrupted. In fact, he'll probably do what he can to get in your way. If he's truly jealous of your rocket ride to the top of the company, he may do what he can to slow you down. Whether he's bold enough to sabotage your records, or he just makes you late for a meeting, he's not giving his 100 percent support to you.

Aren't you tired of not being able to tell him about your day? Is he still rolling his eyes whenever you have good news? Does he change the conversation from your job story to his?

Are you *playing down* your accomplishments so as not to hurt his feelings?

Dump him fast. You can climb the ladder better without having to carry his dead weight.

He sabotages your diet.

You're working hard and you're succeeding. You've lost ten pounds already through sheer effort, determination, and willpower.

And he's mad as hell.

If you lose weight, then he's going to have to, otherwise, you'll look better than he does.

If you lose weight, other men will start noticing you, and you're sure to want someone else.

If you lose weight, then he has to give up the hold he has over you in that department.

He has a million reasons why he wants to keep you the way you were. And the very least of them might just be that he doesn't *think* about the fact that you're avoiding fat and sugar. It's not enough of a presence in his mind that you've been working on a goal. He's single-focused: Stock the fridge with the junk food I like. What's with all this watermelon?

If he can't snap out of it and support you in your goals, then you'd lose 180 pounds or so just by dumping him.

He downplays your accomplishments to play up his own.

You got a raise? So what. So did he. Of course, his was only fifty cents more per hour, but it's still a raise.

You were voted president of your association? He was president of four associations when he was back in school, and they still call him and ask for his advice today.

You made a great soufflé today? He *invented* soufflés.

What's with this guy? He can't remove himself from your stories long enough to just be happy for you. He's measuring himself against you, doing anything to knock you down so he'll look better by comparison.

He's quite supportive, isn't he?

Dump him. He'll probably tell you he's been dumped *better* before.

You're having bad dreams.

Hey, even your *subconscious* wants this guy gone, so take the hint.

Forget about all the Freudian stuff of dreams, how what you dream of can be what you want as well as don't want. If in your dreams he turns into a big rat or a monster of scary proportions, if his belongings all morph into snakes, his gifts to you burst into flames, the necklace he gave you turns into a noose . . . your brain is trying to tell you something.

Either that or you had bad clams.

Your blood pressure is up, you can't sleep, you're a wreck.

He's making you *physically sick* now, is he? The stress he causes you day after day can take a big toll on your health and actually shave years off your life.

Being with him is *killing* you.

Dump him.

His family comes first.

If it's a choice between going to your family's Thanksgiving dinner or his, his family always wins. Christmas? His family has unbreakable traditions (like yours doesn't?) and it's either you go to his place or he sulks all weekend at yours.

He's set up a ranking system, and you and yours aren't in the top five.

Give yourself a great Christmas gift. Dump him and go home for the holidays.

He's not nice to his mother and his sisters.

He's mean and ungrateful to his mother.

He treats his sisters with such disrespect that it goes far beyond normal sibling squabbling.

This is a man who does not like women. He may have a thousand reasons for why his mom isn't the prime candidate for Mother of the Year, and his sisters may have tormented him during his growing-up years. But when a man reaches adulthood, he should learn to treat the women in his life well. And his mom and sisters helped form his way of interacting with women.

So if he's a snarling brat with his mom and sis, he probably isn't the most sensitive, loving guy in the world. And he'd probably forget you on Mother's Day someday as well.

His family is not nice to you.

His family never warmed to you.

Sure they're cordial and they invite you to family parties, but there's still such a distance left there. You're not comfortable hugging them good-bye, and they're not comfortable hugging you hello. You get the distinct feeling that they have an unflattering nickname for you, and you're sure your guy wouldn't call them on it.

Just having an insensitive family isn't grounds to dump an otherwise wonderful guy, but if he's joining in on skewering you at the family dinner table, if he won't stand up for you, then leave him to them.

It's just that many fewer birthday cards you'll have to send, and absolutely no difference in the number of birthday cards you'll receive from them.

He doesn't share the bills.

He's one of those guys who tells you he'll pick up the tab next time. He'll give you money for his phone calls on the bill next week. He's always promising to pay you back for ordering the fight on your pay-per-view, but you know you'd have a better chance of knocking out Tyson yourself than of getting that cash.

Your guy's a sponge. He's letting you foot the bill for all of the things he's enjoying because of you, not with you.

It's fine for you to pay whenever you'd like, but when you're reluctantly pulling out your credit card because you're expected to pay all the time, then it's time to get a table for one.

Dump him and spend the money on yourself. At least you'd say thank you.

You're always having to hear yourself say, "But what about *my* needs?"

Listen to yourself!

Do you sound like the stereotypical whiny girlfriend? Are you listening from within yourself and can't believe how much of a nag you've become?

Are you begging him to give you what you need?

Do you hate the sound of your own voice?

When he's so bad you've become someone *you* can't even stand, it's time to get out and find your old self again.

You want romance and you're not getting it.

His idea of romance is sitting on the couch and letting you talk to him during a blackout. There's no TV, after all, so you might as well. Isn't he a dream?

Maybe he used to bring home flowers and sing you songs, caress your shoulders and feed you chocolate-covered strawberries. But he grew out of that.

Maybe he was never the type for grand gestures and sweet nothings.

The ultrasweet stuff does fade over time, but he should be able to romance you time and again. It should occur to him that you might enjoy a back rub or a candlelight dinner once in a while. It should occur to him that he could treat you to a few little indulgences.

What's romantic? He doesn't need to give you balloon rides over wine country, a magnum of champagne and violin serenades. He could just make up a little poem for you, bring you a little trifle because he was thinking of you, play romantic music on the stereo and twirl you around the living room for just a few minutes. He could just touch your face and look into your eyes like he used to. It doesn't take much.

But if he's just not interested, even when you *demand* a little attention, drop him. Give him a grand gesture he'll never forget.

The thrill is gone.

You don't get tingles anymore when he touches you.

You're not glad to hear his voice on the other end of the phone line.

His kiss is just a kiss.

The earth does not move.

Face it. The thrill is gone. And if you can't get it back, even after tons of effort and exercises and games, it's just gone.

Let it go.

He gets jealous when you drool over Mel Gibson.

You're watching a Mel movie, and he gets mad when he hears your *breathing change*. He argues, "You're getting excited over seeing his butt, aren't you?" You are, naturally, but you have to appease your guy and you wind up missing the second butt shot. Or any close-up of those eyes.

Your guy can't handle it if you admire any man but him. He just may feel he has a real chance of losing you to Mel Gibson.

He gets mad, clams up, and gives you the silent treatment, and the next thing you know he's erased all the Mel Gibson movies you have in your home video collection. Even *Bird on a Wire*.

All you can do is send him and his Pamela Anderson Lee posters packing.

You don't want him around to interfere if Mel Gibson might be available. Or at the very least, you'll be free to enjoy those butt shots and those eyes.

His voice unnerves you.

He starts talking and all you're thinking is, "Will you just *shut up*?!"

You've actually grown tired of hearing him talk. The pitch of his voice hits a point in your spine and gives you the chills. Not the good kind, either.

When he comes through the house, calling you to come help him do something, you'd rather hide under the bed than let him find you. And if you're *hiding under the bed* from him, I'd say that's a pretty good sign you're not meant to be with him.

You'd prefer silence.

It's just something about the sound his voice makes that drives you nuts. And not in a good way.

When you'd rather listen to anything but him, it's time to move on.

He treats you like a child.

He gets a tone in his voice that most people use only with little kids. It's not an adorable baby talk voice. It's condescending. It's talking to you from his higher station in life. It's talking down to you.

You have to ask his permission.

He's got a judgment for everything you do.

He calls you Kiddo.

He asks you to call him Daddy.

Tell this guy to go get himself a doll and leave you alone.

Dump him, baby.

You just don't *look* right in pictures.

You just don't look like you belong together. Nobody matches you up in the "who belongs to whom" game at very lame parties and office retreats. It looks like somebody spliced together all your couple pictures, putting his head on another man's body. You just don't see it. It just doesn't mesh.

Your names don't even sound right together. Couples' names usually run together in their minds and the minds of their friends and family. Almost any names, when said together, start to sound like they belong together. (Try it with your own friends.)

But not your names. It just doesn't work. It's awkward. It's a sign.

You'd rather be alone.

He asks to come over, and you'd rather be alone.

He wants to go out tonight, and you'd rather stay home by yourself.

He offers to stay after the party and help clean up, and you tell him not to.

You'd just rather be alone.

And when that happens on Valentine's Day, you can be sure you'd rather be alone than be with him anytime.

Stop hiding out alone behind your closed shades. Dump him and get a life again.

He puts his car before you.

If your guy had $1,000, what would he do with it? If buying car parts ranks higher on the list than anything having to do with you, then you're the Other Woman. His car is his lady. He's probably named her and speaks about her like she's a person you both know.

If you got stuck in a hailstorm and he had one umbrella, would he protect your head or her hood?

Does he have more pictures of his car in his wallet than pictures of you?

Is there a framed picture of his car by his bed where yours used to be?

He won't pick you up from work because he just washed the car and doesn't want it to get dirty just yet?

He caresses his car like he hasn't caressed you in years?

He talks about you in car terms, like "getting under your hood?"

His being a car lover is one thing, but if he's more in love with his car than with you, trade him in for a new model.

He hates children.

He calls them rug rats and ankle biters, and he means it.

He doesn't think your friend's kids are cute, and he'd rather die than go to a baby shower with you.

He doesn't talk to kids or let babies hold his finger. He doesn't offer to hold the baby when a quick handoff is needed.

Some guys are just not baby-oriented if they don't have one of their own. But there's a difference between not wanting to hold the baby because he's afraid he might drop it and not wanting to hold the baby because he can't stand her. He makes faces. He *tsks* when asked to help. He ignores you when you tell him to look at that adorable baby in the shopping cart.

And kids can tell when a person isn't into them. Even a newborn knows your guy is a big jerk!

If the guy doesn't have a place in his heart for kids, his heart is too small.

Dump him.

Children hate him.

Normally, kids love any adult who acknowledges them, spends time with them, or plays with them. But kids are smart. They're perceptive.

If a nine-year-old rejects your guy's offer to go out and build a tree fort, if your nephew turns down an offer to go get some Happy Meals, if the kids run the other way and make their oh-so-subtle jokes when your guy comes around, then there's something wrong.

Does he make the baby cry just by being in the room? Does the two-year-old call him Meanie?

Sure, kids can be cruel about appearances, but when they just can't stand your guy, give it a thought. Why does he frighten small children?

He lives in the past.

The guy lives in his old high school football team jersey. His place looks like a teenage boy's bedroom.

He talks about "the glory days of '82" when his life was perfect. Ah, sweet nostalgia. A little trip down memory lane is a wonderful vacation, but you can't pitch a tent and live there. If your guy is miserable in the here and now, if he's just pining for the old days when he was a god and everyone wanted to be him, then maybe you would have been perfect together . . . in a past life.

Make him part of *your* ancient history.

He's helpless.

He can't do anything for himself.

He waits for you to cook dinner, even though he's been home since four and could have done it himself.

He leaves the shopping to you.

He leaves the chores and responsibilities to you.

He plays wounded puppy when it's time to get the ketchup stain out of his shirt: "But I don't know how to do it. *You* do it for me."

He can't get his own mom a birthday card. You have to do it.

He doesn't know how to call and book airline tickets. You do it.

Do you want to spend all your time taking care of him and doing all of his work?

Is "helpless" on your list of top ten admirable qualities in your dream man?

Either he learns how to make a sandwich or he's outta there.

He's overly dramatic.

Everything is a much bigger deal to him than it is to everyone else.

His life is the epicenter of unfairness. Unbelievable things happen to him, and his reactions to all of them are worthy of an Oscar. He's not upset, he's *livid*. He's not sad, he's *devastated*. He's not happy, he's *ecstatic*.

He can't just tell you something. It has to be a big speech, complete with flourishes and lots of pounding for emphasis.

And when he gets mad, look out. He wants to rant and rave and pace through the house. He wants to scream at the top of his lungs and throw a complete tantrum.

He's a regular person turned up to level ten. He's just so intense.

Tell him to bring it down a level or he can exit stage left.

He has no emotions.

He's not a guy who feels things. It takes a lot to make him laugh, and he wouldn't cry if you paid him.

Sad movies don't even affect him. He just shrugs and says, "It's just a movie."

You can't tell his happy face from his sad face, and his tender look could also be rage. The man is an android. He has no emotions chip.

Some people call him strong and serious, others ask you if he's in shock.

Call it being thick-skinned, call it being impervious to outside matters or inside feelings. Sounds like a dead tree to me.

Dump him.

You're the least bit afraid of him.

If he frightens you even a little bit, just get out of there.
Don't even take the time to dump him.
Just leave.

He sympathizes with bad guys.

Adulterers, tax cheats, bad guys in general. He doesn't
think they deserve what they get when they're caught. He
scoffs at jail sentences, believes these guys were just doing
what they could to get ahead. He sympathizes with various
evildoers who make the evening news.

Think hard about where his beliefs system lies.

It's much better to be with the good guys.

You have to drag him away from the computer.

Or any other toy he'd rather play with than you.

He can sit in front of that screen for hours, and he can't tear himself away long enough to acknowledge that you're in the room. He has no idea what time of day it is, or even what day it is. He'll tell you to hold on and wait for him, just until he gets to the next level . . . and then the next . . . and then the next. . . .

He has better conversations, is more open and honest, in an online chat room than he does with you.

Dump him via his E-mail, or send him an Instant Message after you've moved out.

He's beyond help.

You know that you're not supposed to take on a guy the way a real estate investor would take on a fixer-upper. But you thought he had potential. You thought that with a little bit of work, he could have been a contender.

Well, you were wrong.

It's a lost cause, a futile effort.

Put this little project to rest, and get rid of him. A better opportunity is just around the corner.

You've had better offers.

And if *every* offer is a better offer, perhaps you should stop declining. It's just time to undo the shackles and take part in what's available to you.

You feel empty inside.

If you stopped to think about it, you'd realize it's been a long time since you felt some real excitement. Your day-to-day life is just running together; everything's routine, everything's the way it always is. You haven't felt joy and contented bliss in your life in a long time.

You feel like your soul has been asleep.

And when you wake yours up to taste life again, you'll see how unhappy you've allowed your world to become. If your guy wants to wake up his soul as well, to slip out of your comfortable patterns and share some new experiences, that's great. If he'd rather just keep it all status quo, with barely a pulse, think twice.

Can you really live your life like that?

Are you all empty inside right now? Will he wake up and join you, or not?

Everyone's always saying, "What do you see in him?"

The people who know you best can't figure out why you're with a guy like him. He's so not-your-type.

Everyone gives you that strange look while you're tap-dancing around why he's the guy for you, and then they shrug and say, "Whatever makes you happy." How inspiring.

"As long as he treats you right" is what they settle on, if not "Have you seen him in daylight yet?"

You know you're missing something when everyone's still trying to set you up with other guys and if their first words to you at the family reunion are, "So, did you dump that other guy yet?"

The people who know you best know that this is not the guy for you. They know you can do much better, and as much as they'll tell you that to your face, they feel it even more in their hearts.

You know you deserve better.

You may have been secretly wishing he were different, more like another guy, more romantic, more dependable. It's certainly popped into your head that you could do far better than you're doing right now, and you could be far happier with a better person. Or even alone.

Think about what you want, and if your guy doesn't match up, dump him.

You can do far better.

You know he isn't "The One."

You believe that everyone has someone out there somewhere who's meant just for them, and deep in your heart, you know that this guy is just not your destiny. He's just not what fate had in mind for you. . . .